MW00527757

JULIUS CÆSAR

By WILLIAM SHAKESPEARE

Preface and Annotations by
HENRY N. HUDSON

Introduction by
CHARLES HAROLD HERFORD

Julius Cæsar
By William Shakespeare
Preface and Annotations by Henry N. Hudson
Introduction by Charles Harold Herford

Print ISBN 13: 978-1-4209-5274-2
eBook ISBN 13: 978-1-4209-5275-9

This edition copyright © 2016. Digireads.com Publishing.

All rights reserved. No part of this publication may be reproduced, distributed, or transmitted in any form or by any means, including photocopying, recording, or other electronic or mechanical methods, without the prior written permission of the publisher, except in the case of brief quotations embodied in critical reviews and certain other noncommercial uses permitted by copyright law.

Cover Image: 'Julius Caesar', Act III, Scene 2, Marc Antony's Oration (oil on canvas), Sullivan, William Holmes (1836-1908) / Royal Shakespeare Company Collection, Stratford-upon-Avon, Warwickshire / Bridgeman Images.

Please visit *www.digireads.com*

CONTENTS

Preface

First printed in the folio of 1623, and one of the best-printed plays in that inestimable volume; the text being in so clear and sound a state, that editors have but little trouble about it. The date of the composition has been variously argued, some placing it in the middle period of the Poet's labours, others among the latest; and, as no clear contemporary notice or allusion had been produced, the question could not be positively determined. It is well known that the original *Hamlet* must have been written as early as 1602; and in iii. 2 of that play Polonius says "I did enact Julius Cæsar: I was killed in the Capitol; Brutus killed me." As the play now in hand lays the scene of the stabbing in the Capitol, it is not improbable, to say the least, that the Poet had his own *Julius* Cæsar in mind when he wrote the passage in *Hamlet.* And that such was the case is made further credible by the fact, that Polonius speaks of himself as having enacted the part when he "play'd once in the University," and that in the title-page of the first edition of *Hamlet* we have the words, "As it hath been divers times acted in the city of London; as also in the two Universities of Cambridge and Oxford." Still the point cannot be affirmed with certainty; for there were several earlier plays on the subject, and especially a Latin play on Cæsar's death, which was performed at Oxford in 1582.

Collier argued that Shakespeare's play must have been on the stage before 1603, his reason being as follows. Drayton's *Mortimeriados* appeared in 1596. The poem was afterwards recast by the author, and published again in 1603 as *The Barons' Wars.* The recast has the following lines, which were not in the original form of the poem:

> Such one he was, of him we boldly say,
> In whose rich soul all sovereign powers did suit,
> In whom in peace *the elements all lay*
> *So mix'd*, as none could sovereignty impute:
> That't seem'd, when Heaven his model first began,
> In him it show'd *perfection in a man.*

Here we have a striking resemblance to what Antony says of Brutus in the play:

> His life was gentle; and *the elements*
> *So mix'd in him*, that *Nature* might stand up
> And say to all the world, *This was a man!*

Collier's theory is, that Drayton, before recasting his poem, had either seen the play in manuscript or heard it at the theatre, and so caught and copied the language of Shakespeare.

I confess there does not seem to me any great strength in this argument; for the idea and even the language of the resembling lines was so much a commonplace in the Poet's time, that no one could claim any special right of authorship in it. Nevertheless it is now pretty certain that the play was written as early as 1601, Mr. Halliwell having lately produced the following from Weever's *Mirror of Martyrs*, which was printed that year:

> The many-headed multitude were drawn
> By Brutus' speech, that Cæsar was ambitious:
> When eloquent Mark Antony had shown
> His virtues, who but Brutus then was vicious?

As there is nothing in the history that could have suggested this, we can only ascribe it to some acquaintance with the play: so that the passage may be justly regarded as decisive of the question.

The style alone of the drama led me to rest in about the same conclusion long ago. For it seems to me that in *Julius Cæsar* the diction is more gliding and continuous, and the imagery more round and amplified, than in the dramas known to have been of the Poet's latest period But these distinctive notes are of a nature to be more easily felt than described; and to make them felt examples will best serve. Take, then, a sentence from the soliloquy of Brutus just after he has pledged himself to the conspiracy:

> 'Tis a common proof,
> That lowliness is young ambition's ladder,
> Whereto the climber-upward turns his face;
> But, when he once attains the upmost round,
> He then unto the ladder turns his back,
> Looks in the clouds, scorning the base degrees
> By which he did ascend.

Here we have a full, rounded period in which all the elements seem to have been adjusted, and the whole expression set in order, before any part of it was written down. The beginning foresees the end, the end remembers the beginning, and the thought and image are evolved together in an even continuous flow. The thing is indeed perfect in its way, still it is not in Shakespeare's latest and highest style. Now compare with this a passage from *The Winter's Tale*:

> When you speak, sweet,
> I'd have you do it ever: when you sing,
> I'd have you buy and sell so; so give alms;

Pray so; and for the ordering your affairs,
To sing them too: when you do dance, I wish you
A wave o' the sea, that you might ever do
Nothing but that; move still, still so, and own
No other function.

Here the workmanship seems to make and shape itself as it goes along, thought kindling thought, and image prompting image, and each part neither concerning itself with what has gone before, nor what is coming after. The very sweetness has a certain piercing quality, and we taste it from clause to clause, almost from word to word, as so many keen darts of poetic rapture shot forth in rapid succession. Yet the passage, notwithstanding its swift changes of imagery and motion, is perfect in unity and continuity.

Such is, I believe, a fair illustration of what has long been familiar to me as the supreme excellence of Shakespeare's ripest, strongest, and most idiomatic style. *Antony and Cleopatra* is pre-eminently rich in this quality; but there is enough of it in *The Tempest, The Winter's Tale, Coriolanus,* and *Cymbeline,* to identify them as belonging to the same stage and period of authorship. But I can find hardly so much as an earnest of it in *Julius Cæsar*; and nothing short of very strong positive evidence would induce me to class this drama with those, as regards the time of writing.

The historic materials of the play were drawn from *The Life of Julius Cæsar, The Life of Marcus Brutus,* and *The Life of Marcus Antonius,* as set forth in Sir Thomas North's translation of Plutarch. This work, aptly described by Warton as "Shakespeare's storehouse of learned history," was first printed in 1579, and reprinted in 1595, 1603, and 1612, not to mention several later editions. The translation was avowedly made, not directly from the Greek, but from the French version of Jaques Amiot, Bishop of Auxerre. The book is among our richest and freshest literary monuments of that age; and, apart from the use made of it by Shakespeare, is in itself an invaluable repertory of honest, manly, idiomatic English. In most of the leading incidents of the play, the charming old Greek is minutely followed; though in divers cases those incidents are worked out with surpassing fertility of invention and art. But, besides this, in many places the Plutarchian form and order of thought, and also the very words of North's racy and delectable old English, are retained.

It may be well to add, that on the 13th of February, B.C. 44, the feast of Lupercalia was held, when the crown was offered to Cæsar by Antony. On the 15th of March following, Cæsar was slain. In November, B.C. 43, the Triumvirs, Octavius, Antony, and Lepidus, met on a small island near Bononia, and there made up their bloody proscription. The overthrow of Brutus and Cassius, near Philippi, took

place in the Fall of the next year. So that the events of the drama cover
a period of something over two years and a half.

                                                                HENRY N. HUDSON

Introduction

Julius Cæsar was first published in the Folio of 1623. The
Cambridge editors justly emphasise the extreme correctness of the text
there given, and conjecture that this play 'may have been (as the
preface falsely implied that all were) printed from the original MS. of
the author.' It was entered in the Stationers' Register, November 8,
1623, among the plays of Shakespeare 'not formerly entered to other
men,' and then first published.

The most important evidence for the date of *Julius Cæsar* is the
following passage in Weever's *Mirror of Martyrs, or the Life and
Death of Sir John Oldcastle* (printed in 1601):—

> The many-headed multitude were drawn
>   By Brutus' speech, that Cæsar was ambitious.
> When eloquent Mark Antonie had shewn
>   His virtues, who but Brutus then was vicious?

Shakespeare's only known source, Plutarch, merely mentions the
funeral speech of Brutus; summarises Antony's in three lines of quite a
different purport; and knows nothing of the 'many-headed multitude's'
ready change of front, exhibited with peculiarly Shakespearean sarcasm
in the play. The inference is forcible that Shakespeare's *Julius Cæsar*
was already familiar to the stage when Weever wrote. Weever,
however, tells us that his *Mirror* was 'some two years ago [*i.e.* in 1599]
made fit for print.' The style and metre of *Julius Cæsar* are compatible
enough with the date of *Henry V.*[1] But its close and numerous links
between our play and *Hamlet* speak for the date 1600-1; and the lost
play of *Cæsar's Fall* on which, in 1602, Webster, Middleton, Munday,
Drayton, were at work for the rival company would have been a
somewhat tardy counterblast to an old piece of 1599. Other signs of the
deep impression it made point to the later date. *Julius Cæsar* was
certainly not unconcerned in the revival of the fashion for tragedies of
revenge with a ghost in them, which suddenly set in with Marston's
Antonio and Mellida and Chettle's *Hoffman* in 1601. Jonson made his
own fashions. But the sudden appearance of the man of little Latin in
the arena of Roman tragedy put him on his mettle, and there can be

---

[1] With which it is in fact in classed, on purely metrical grounds, by the latest
investigator of Shakespeare's metre, Goswin König (*Der Vers in Sh.'s Dramen*, p. 137).

little doubt that his massive *Sejanus* (1603) conveyed an unavowed challenge.[2] If *Julius Cæsar*, however, greatly stimulated tragedy at large, it struck a blight upon the dramas of Cæsar's death, hitherto a very flourishing growth. After the abortive effort of Henslowe's men, and Alexander's probably quite independent tragedy, printed in Scotland in 1604,[3] no English poet again attempted to vie with Shakespeare. In rude German prose *Julius Cæsar* was repeatedly acted by the comedians abroad.[4] A puppet-play, doubtless founded on the drama, is mentioned in 1605. A century later the Duke of Buckingham divided the play into two tragedies, *Cæsar* and *Brutus*, neither of which was ever performed.[5] And in Voltaire's *Brutus* and *La Mort de Cesar* Shakespeare achieved his first (as yet very qualified) triumphs over the dramatic traditions of the Continent.

The suggestion that *Julius Cæsar* was prompted by the conspiracy of Essex in January to February 1601 (Furnivall, *Acad.*, September 18, 1875, and Preface to *Leopold Shakspere*) is interesting, but the links are far too slender to support any inference as to the date.

As has just been stated, the *Fall of Cæsar* was familiar on English stages before Shakespeare wrote, as well as the kindred subject of Cæsar and Pompey,—a kind of First Part to the History. The very early (and perhaps mythical) *Julius Cæsar* recorded to have been performed at Whitehall in 1562 possibly included both. A lost play, *Cæsar Interfectus*, by Dr. Eedes, was acted at Oxford in 1582. Gosson mentions a *Cæsar and Pompey* in his *School of Abuse* (1579), and Henslowe another in his Diary (1594). None of these survives, but Shakespeare seems to be cognisant of their existence. His opening scene is addressed to a public familiar with the history of Pompey and Pompey's sons;[6] Polonius' description of his performance of the murdered Cæsar at the University, indicates that that subject was in vogue there; and some apparently purposeless deviations from Plutarch are probably concessions to an established dramatic or literary tradition. Thus the famous 'Et tu Brute' had occurred in the *True Tragedy* (1595); and Chaucer already placed the murder in the Capitol instead of in Pompey's Curia, though Shakespeare still makes Cæsar's bleeding body lie along the base of Pompey's statue.

But Shakespeare undoubtedly drew his materials substantially from Plutarch's lives of Cæsar, Brutus, and Antony, as translated by Sir

---

[2] It will suffice to mention here Mr. Fleay's belief that Jonson abridged and corrected *Julius Cæsar* into its present form in 1607 (still affirmed his *Life of Shakespeare*, p. 214).

[3] *Julius Cæsar*, by William Alexander, afterwards Earl of Stirling. It was republished in London, 1607. It is a learned work.

[4] First at Dresden, 1626 (Creizenach, *Schausfiele d.engl. Com.* p. xlii).

[5] *The Tragedy of Cæsar* and *The Tragedy of Brutus*, both printed 1722. Their relation to the original has been elaborately handled by O. Mielck, *J. B.* xxiv. 27 f.

[6] Similarly v. 1. 102 implies familiarity with the suicide of Cato.

Thomas North.[7] The translations had probably become as early familiar to him, and interested him as keenly, as the nearly contemporary folio of Holinshed.[8] In now closing his Holinshed and opening his Plutarch Shakespeare turned from a homely though picturesque annalist to a philosophic and sentimental biographer, from a naive chronicler of events to a literary and self-conscious exponent of men. For Plutarch personality was, if not the supreme, certainly the most attractive and intelligible factor in history; public events interested him by their bearing upon character, and his peculiar art and charm lay in following his heroes among the intimacies of their private life, and allowing them to reveal themselves in their familiar converse, their table-talk, their memorable epigrams and repartees. He had, moreover, the moralist's eye for ethical problems, for conflicts of motive and passion and conscience. And neither of these traits can have been without relish for an intellect ripening towards the profounder psychology and the graver questionings of *Measure for Measure*, *Hamlet*, and *Cæsar*. Hence, while Holinshed had furnished little more than the outline of the action to *Richard III.* or *Richard II.*, the far subtler tragic conflict of Brutus, with almost every detail of the action, and a hundred vivid traits of character, are already clearly foreshadowed in Plutarch. But it is in the drama that the implicit eloquence of the subject is first revealed. The means by which this is effected are, however, wonderfully simple. The language, though charged with poetry, is of a pellucid simplicity which Shakespeare had rarely approached; and through large tracts of it Plutarch's pedestrian narrative survives, only lifted to a higher potency and purged of the last suggestion of banality and rhetoric. But at a few decisive points Shakespeare intervenes. Brutus' monologue in ii. 1. is wholly original. Of his oration after Cæsar's death, Plutarch records merely that it was designed 'to win the favour of the people and to justify that they had done.'[9] Shakespeare gives him a speech strikingly unlike any of his other speeches in style, though full of his character;[10]

---

[7] *The Lives of the Noble Grecians, compared together by that grave learned philosopher and historiographer* PLUTARKE OF CHAERONIA. As the title page candidly states, North had translated the French translation of Amyot, to which his own owes something of its relative accomplishment, as prose, and a few errors (*e.g.* Decius for Decimus Brutus). North is reprinted in the *Tudor Translations*, and the Lives in question in Hazlitt's *Shakspeare's Library*. There is an exhaustive study of Shakespeare's use of Plutarch by Delius in J. *B*. xvii. 67.

[8] Bassanio's comparison of Portia to her namesake 'Cato's daughter, Brutus' Portia' (*Mer. of Ven.* i. 1. 166); Portia's own name; and the deep admiration for Cæsar betrayed by a host of earlier allusions all indicate this.

[9] Even these words strictly describe a previous harangue on the Capitol.

[10] The style of *Brutus' speech* was evidently adopted on Plutarch's hint that *in writing Greek* he affected 'the brief compendious manner of speech of the Lacedæmonians'; writing *e.g.* to the Pergamenians: 'I understand you have given Dolabella money; if you have done it willingly, you confess you have offended me; if against your wills, show it then by giving me willingly.' The model of such a speech, in a

a speech moreover in prose,[11] which he nowhere else uses. Antony's oration is represented by the following:—

'When Cæsar's body was brought into the marketplace, Antonius making his funeral Oration in praise of the dead according to the ancient custom of Rome, and perceiving that his words moved the common people to compassion: he framed his eloquence to make their hearts yearn the more, and taking Cæsar's gown all bloudy in his hand, he layed it open to the sight of them all, shewing what a number of cuts and holes it had in it. Therewith all the people fell presently into such a rage and mutinie that there was no more order kept among the common people.'[12]

Plutarch assures us that Antony was eloquent: but he left it to Shakespeare to convert his blunt Casca-like report into the superb

> You all do know this mantle: I remember
> The first time ever Cæsar put it on, etc.

The action of the play is strikingly clear and simple. In this point of dramatic technique, as in others, it differs widely from the other Roman plays. The bewildering complexity of the history of Antony and Cleopatra has its counterpart in that play. A like chaos on a smaller scale filled the period intervening between Cæsar's death and Philippi, and Plutarch patiently chronicles the undecisive movements and counter-movements which for a while held destiny in suspense: the negotiations between the conspirators and the Senate, its vote of thanks to Brutus and Antonius, the feud between Antony and Octavius, and Brutus' voluntary withdrawal from Italy—not for his own safety, but foreseeing the overthrow of Rome; his sojourn at Athens, where he 'went daily to hear philosophic lectures'; his quixotic humanities in the field and reiterated dissensions with Cassius; finally the two battles at Philippi, three weeks apart, in which Cassius and Brutus were separately vanquished. All this Shakespeare compresses into three critical moments:—Cæsar's funeral, and the final ruin of Brutus and

---

parallel situation, Shakespeare had at hand, as Mr. Gollancz has plausibly suggested, in the harangue of Belleforest's Hamlet to the people after killing the king (cf. also Kuno Fischer, *Hamlet*, p. 104). One more of the inexhaustible points of contact between the two plays, and one more indication that Belleforest was known to Shakespeare, though the first attested English edition is of 1608.

[11] Why did Shakespeare make Brutus here use prose? The question is excellently answered by Janssen (*Die Prosa in Sh's Dramen*, p. 41). Brutus is an idealist. He loves 'the people' in idea, but is constrained when addressing them face to face. He has eloquence and passion for Antony; but, unlike Antony, only the dry language of understanding for the mob. The words "Peace, freedom and liberty," stick in his throat, and he gives them instead a mathematical demonstration of his honesty.'

[12] *Life of J. Cæsar* (Hazlitt: Shakspeare Library, vol. iii. p. 186). A similar but less detailed passage occurs in his *Life of M. Antony*, ib. p. 331.

Cassius in Italy; the camp at Sardis, and their quarrel; Philippi, and their overthrow. The quarrel (iv. 3.) is a wonderful example of concentration. Plutarch reports very briefly how on their first meeting 'they went into a little chamber together and bade every man avoid, and did shut the doors to them. Then they began to pour out their complaints one to the other, and grew hot and loud, earnestly accusing one another, and at length fell both a weeping.' In the height of their strife they are interrupted by the 'counterfeit Cynic,' Phaonius (the Poet of the play). On the following day they again meet and exchange grave reproaches: Brutus has condemned and noted Lucius Pella; Cassius remonstrates; Brutus bids him remember the Ides of March; but neither now passes the limits of debate. Finally, on the closing page of the Life, Plutarch records the death of Portia. All these four strands are interwoven in Shakespeare's wonderful scene. The 'hot and loud complaints' and 'weeping' of their first meeting are made articulate with the arguments of their second. The intrusion of the Cynic, instead of 'breaking off their strife for that time,' throws a gleam of relieving burlesque upon their restored harmony; and the tidings of Portia's death, undermining the sources of Brutus' Stoic self-control, give the clue to the uncontrolled outburst, as anger, of the passion so sternly suppressed as grief. 'I did not think you could have been so angry,' says Cassius, and his anger is as amazing to the reader as it is to Cassius, until this subtle trait renders it natural and pathetic.

Plutarch's character-drawing, like his narrative, suffers from his twofold role of historian and moralist. His Brutus is a compromise between the humane idealist whom he wished to portray and the grasping *doctrinaire* whom he was too honest wholly to efface. His lofty Stoic condescends to a vulgar rivalry with Cassius for the election to the praetor's chair; nay, at Pharsalia, the general whose humanity amazed friend and foe promises his soldiers 'the sack of two cities if they fought like men,'—an embarrassing inconsistency for which his biographer rather awkwardly apologises as the 'only fault to be found in all Brutus' life, and that is not to be gainsaid.' The faults of Shakespeare's Brutus are exposed with a far surer hand; he is nevertheless a loftier character: no soil of meanness, cruelty, or vulgar rivalry complicates the tragedy of his fate. The personal relation to Cæsar which he violates 'for the general' (good) is a more intimate one. Rome calls him 'Cæsar's angel.' In Plutarch, Cæsar 'did not trust him overmuch,' and included him with Cassius in his dislike of 'lean and whitely-faced' men. Brutus on his part was 'incensed' by Cassius against the tyrant. The monologue which Shakespeare puts in his mouth is a marvel of fanatical self-deception. It is not any actual 'tyranny' that moves him, for he owns that 'the quarrel will bear no colour for the thing' Cæsar 'is'; it is not even the abstract name of king which moves him, but a 'change of nature' which that might induce. 'Then lest it may, prevent.' Brutus, like Hamlet, is set in action by the bidding of a ghost; but his ghost is not the discloser of a crying wrong which he groans to be summoned to set right, but a true phantom which drives him headlong to the redress of wrongs which even his biassed reason can only discover in a hypothetical futurity.

Shakespeare's Cassius is, to a far greater degree than his Brutus, Plutarch made eloquent. The contrast between the philosophic and the self-seeking politician appealed strongly to the Greek's academic intellect, and he brings it out with incisive sharpness. He admits that Brutus' tactics were disastrous to the conspirators and to the republican cause. But he has no eye for the pathos of Cassius' devotion to the friend whose errors he recognised and suffered by. This trait Shakespeare has sympathetically seized in the famous 'quarrel scene'; Cassius' hot temper blazes rashly out; but Brutus' answering passion overwhelms him with grief and despair—

> Come, Antony, and young Octavius, come,
> For Cassius is aweary of the world.

But the brilliant figure of Antony owes far more to Shakespeare. Plutarch's Antony is a scheming soldier, who carries his way by practical sagacity and ruthless cruelty. Shakespeare's is in addition to all this a consummate artist, and an artist by temperament as well as by his technical mastery of effect. Shakespeare has deliberately charged his eloquence with the task of inflaming the people which Plutarch's Antony achieves mainly by strategic skill He even aggravates the difficulty of the task to throw into relief the intellectual brilliance of the achievement. The Roman multitude, in Plutarch, need little incitement to rise upon the slayers of Cæsar. The first act of the conspirators is to take refuge in the Capitol; when Brutus at last ventures down, and addresses the people, they 'showed, immediately after, that they were not at all contented with the murder.' The next day, by Antony's arrangement, Cæsar's will is read to them, and they are 'marvellously sorry for him.' The funeral oration which Antony then delivers has but to fire a train, not to turn a tide.

If Shakespeare idealises Brutus, Cassius, Antony, he has notoriously depressed Cæsar. Plutarch's own Cæsar is far from being the Cæsar of Mommsen; and Shakespeare has touched the slightly disparaging portrait into something like caricature. He dwells with curious persistence on the physical infirmities of the ageing dictator, and swells their number with others of his own devising,—a falling sickness, a deafness in one ear. He accentuates every trait of superstition,—the touching at the Lupercal, the consultation of the sacrificers, the senile vacillation on the morning of the fatal Ides. Above all, he puts in the mouth of the man whose will has just responded so sensitively to the beck of dreams and omens, the most magnificent and sincere professions of immovable constancy. All critics of the play have felt that this caustic treatment of Cæsar needed explanation. The early commentators found one, readily enough, in Shakespeare's limited classical knowledge; and one of his recent biographers has reinforced it, late in the day, with a splendid but irrelevant picture of the real Cæsar.[13] But it is certain that Shakespeare did not think meanly of the 'foremost man in all the world.' Others have suggested more plausibly that Cæsar is presented as he appeared to the conspirators. Certainly he at times seems to justify Cassius' jaundiced vision of him in his weaker moments.[14] But what may hold of Cassius certainly does not hold of Brutus. His Cæsar has no personal faults, and he has never 'known when his affections sway'd more than his reason'; his Cæsar is doomed for what he might become, not for what he is. Brutus alone distinguishes between the man Cæsar and what he stood for. At the outset he would gladly spare the man if he could annihilate the spirit. 'O, that we then could come by Cæsar's spirit, and not dismember Cæsar!' It is his fatal illusion to believe that Cæsar's spirit will perish when Cæsar is dismembered. But Cæsar is no sooner dead than the tokens accumulate that Cæsarism is still alive; and they seem to be specially addressed to Brutus. 'Let Brutus be Cæsar!' cry the mob when he has spoken, confuting him by their very applause. When he looks on the dead body of Cassius his eyes are opened, and the thrilling cry that breaks from him—

> O Julius Cæsar, thou art mighty yet!
> Thy spirit walks abroad, and turns our swords
> In our own proper entrails—

is the final confession of failure. The apparition of Cæsar's spirit is a visible embodiment of the invisible forces which are controlling the issues of the plot. Shakespeare here finely modified tradition to his own purpose. In the drama, as in Plutarch, the ghost replies to his question, 'I am thy evil spirit.' Shakespeare draws this trivial episode into touch with the very heart of the tragedy by identifying Brutus' evil spirit with 'the ghost of Cæsar.' Thus *Julius Cæsar* at the threshold of the tragic period already betrays that sense of mysterious persistences of spiritual energy which continually emerges in the tragedies and inspires some of their most haunting and thrilling moments;—energy which defies the accident of death—

---

[13] Brandes, *Shakespeare* (E.T.) i. 361 £.

[14] Cassius' story of the swimming-match in Tiber, when Cæsar succumbed with a 'Help me, Cassius, or I sink' (i. 2. 111), is Shakespeare's.

For it is, as the air, invulnerable,
And our vain blows malicious mockery

Brutus'

O Julius Cæsar, thou art mighty yet!

is the pathetic recognition of that which Macbeth divines with his horror-stricken

the time has been
That, when the brains were out, the man would die.

Undoubtedly, however, Shakespeare's wonderful intuition of the potency of Cæsarism was facilitated by positive political prepossessions. He interpreted the Rome of Cæsar by the England of Elizabeth, and the analogy was sufficiently close to supply in a measure the place of genuine historical insight. Elizabeth, like Plutarch's Cæsar, was old and infirm, capricious and vain; her death was imminent and the succession not absolutely sure. The failure of Essex's fatuous rebellion may or may not have occurred when Shakespeare wrote; but in any case the monarchy itself must have seemed to him utterly beyond assault. His picture of the Roman demos is notoriously coloured by the Elizabethan's genial contempt for the masses. Plutarch's People, as we have seen, were far from being a *quantité négligeable* to a clever orator.

CHARLES HAROLD HERFORD

1902.

JULIUS CÆSAR

DRAMATIS PERSONAE

JULIUS CÆSAR, *Roman statesman and general*
OCTAVIUS, *Triumvir after Cæsar's death, later Augustus Cæsar,*
first emperor of Rome
MARK ANTONY, *general and friend of Cæsar, a Triumvir after*
his death
LEPIDUS, *third member of the Triumvirate*
MARCUS BRUTUS, *leader of the conspiracy against Cæsar*
CASSIUS, *instigator of the conspiracy*
CASCA, *conspirator against Cæsar*
TREBONIUS, *conspirator against Cæsar*
CAIUS LIGARIUS, *conspirator against Cæsar*
DECIUS BRUTUS, *conspirator against Cæsar*
METELLUS CIMBER, *conspirator against Cæsar*
CINNA, *conspirator against Cæsar*
CALPURNIA, *wife of Cæsar*
PORTIA, *wife of Brutus*
CICERO, *senator*
PUBLIUS, *senator*
POPILLIUS LAENA, *senator*
FLAVIUS, *tribune*
MARELLUS, *tribune*
CATO, *supporter of Brutus*
LUCILLIUS, *supporter of Brutus*
TITINIUS, *supporter of Brutus*
MESSALA, *supporter of Brutus*
VOLUMNIUS, *supporter of Brutus*
ARTEMIDORUS, *a teacher of rhetoric*
CINNA, *a poet*
VARRUS, *servant to Brutus*
CLITUS, *servant to Brutus*
CLAUDIO, *servant to Brutus*
STRATO, *servant to Brutus*
LUCIUS, *servant to Brutus*
DARDANIUS, *servant to Brutus*
PINDARUS, *servant to Cassius*
The Ghost of Cæsar
A Soothsayer, A Poet, Senators, A Cobbler, A Carpenter, Citizens,
Soldiers, Commoners, Messengers, and Servants

ACT I.

SCENE I.

Rome. A Street.

[*Enter* FLAVIUS, MARELLUS, *and a throng of* CITIZENS.]

FLAVIUS. Hence! home, you idle creatures get you home:
Is this a holiday? what! know you not,
Being mechanical,[1] you ought not walk[2]
Upon a labouring day without the sign
Of your profession?[3]—Speak, what trade art thou?
CARPENTER. Why, sir, a carpenter.
MARELLUS. Where is thy leather apron and thy rule?
What dost thou with thy best apparel on?—
You, sir, what trade are you?
SECOND COMMONER. Truly, sir, in respect of[4] a fine workman, I
am but, as you would say, a cobbler.
MARELLUS. But what trade art thou? answer me directly.[5]
COBBLER. A trade, sir, that, I hope, I may use with a safe conscience;
which is, indeed, sir, a mender of bad soles.
MARELLUS. What trade, thou knave? thou naughty knave, what
trade?
COBBLER. Nay, I beseech you, sir, be not out with me: yet, if you be
out, sir, I can mend you.[6]
MARELLUS. What meanest thou by that? mend me, thou saucy
fellow!
COBBLER. Why, sir, cobble you.
FLAVIUS. Thou art a cobbler, art thou?
COBBLER. Truly, sir, all that I live by is with the awl: I meddle with

---

[1] Shakespeare often uses adjectives with the sense of plural substantives; as *mechanical* here for *mechanics* or *artisans*. So in *Hamlet*, i. 1: "Tell me why this same strict and most observant watch so nightly toils the *subject* of the land." The sense in the text is, "Know ye not that, being mechanics, you ought not," &c.

[2] "Ought not *to* walk," of course. This omission of *to* is not infrequent. So in *The Merchant*, i. 3: "Whose own hard dealing teaches them suspect the thoughts of others."

[3] The Poet here transfers to Rome the English customs and usages of his own time; representing men in the several mechanic trades as having their guilds, with appropriate regulations and badges.

[4] Here, as often, *in respect of* is equivalent to *in comparison with.*

[5] *Cobbler*, it seems, was used of a coarse workman, or a *botcher*, in any mechanical trade. So that the Cobbler's answer does not give the information required.—*Directly* here has the sense of the Latin *directus*; *in a straightforward manner*, or *without evasion.*

[6] Of course there is a play upon the two senses of *out* here. To be *out with* a man is to be *at odds* with him; to be *out at the toes* is to need a mending of one's shoes.

no tradesman's matters, nor women's matters, but with awl. I am, indeed, sir, a surgeon to old shoes; when they are in great danger, I recover them. As proper[7] men as ever trod upon neat's leather[8] have gone upon my handiwork.

FLAVIUS. But wherefore art not in thy shop today?
Why dost thou lead these men about the streets?

COBBLER. Truly, sir, to wear out their shoes, to get myself into more work. But, indeed, sir, we make holiday, to see Cæsar and to rejoice in his triumph.

MARELLUS. Wherefore rejoice? What conquest brings he home?
What tributaries follow him to Rome,
To grace in captive bonds his chariot-wheels?
You blocks, you stones, you worse than senseless things!
O you hard hearts, you cruel men of Rome,
Knew you not Pompey? Many a time and oft
Have you climb'd up to walls and battlements,
To towers and windows, yea, to chimney-tops,
Your infants in your arms,[9] and there have sat
The livelong day, with patient expectation,
To see great Pompey pass the streets of Rome:
And when you saw his chariot but appear,
Have you not made an universal shout,
That[10] Tiber trembled underneath her[11] banks,
To hear the replication[12] of your sounds
Made in her concave shores?
And do you now put on your best attire?
And do you now cull out a holiday?[13]
And do you now strew flowers in his way
That comes in triumph over Pompey's blood?[14]

---

[7] *Proper* for *handsome, goodly,* or *fine.* Commonly so in Shakespeare; at least when used of persons.

[8] *Neat's*-leather is what we call *cowhide* or *calfskin. Neat* was applied to all cattle of the bovine genus. So in *The Winters Tale,* i. 2: "The steer, the heifer, and the calf, are all call'd *neat.*" And the word is still so used in "*neat's-foot* oil."

[9] "Your infants *being* in your arms." Ablative absolute.

[10] *That* with the force of *so that* or *insomuch that.* Often so used by the writers of Shakespeare's time.

[11] In classical usage the divinities of rivers were gods, and not goddesses. Old English usage, however, varies; Drayton making them mostly feminine; Spenser, masculine.

[12] *Replication* for *echo* or *reverberation.*—Here, as often, the infinitive *to hear* is used gerundively, and so is equivalent to *at hearing.*

[13] "Do you cull out this time for a holiday?" is the meaning.

[14] The reference is to the great battle of Munda, in Spain, which took place in March of the preceding year. Cæsar was now celebrating his fifth triumph, which was in honour of his final victory over the Pompeian faction. Cnæus and Sextus, the two sons of Pompey the Great, were leaders in that battle, and Cnæus perished.

Be gone!
Run to your houses, fall upon your knees,
Pray to the gods to intermit[15] the plague
That needs must light on this ingratitude.[16]
FLAVIUS. Go, go, good countrymen, and, for this fault,
Assemble all the poor men of your sort;
Draw them to Tiber banks, and weep your tears
Into the channel, till the lowest stream
Do kiss the most exalted shores[17] of all.

[*Exeunt* CITIZENS.]

See whether their basest metal[18] be not moved;
They vanish tongue-tied in their guiltiness.
Go you down that way towards the Capitol;
This way will I disrobe the images,
If you do find them deck'd with ceremony.[19]
MARELLUS. May we do so?
You know it is the feast of Lupercal.[20]
FLAVIUS. It is no matter; let no images
Be hung with Cæsar's trophies.[21] I'll about,
And drive away the vulgar[22] from the streets:
So do you too, where you perceive them thick.
These growing feathers pluck'd from Cæsar's wing
Will make him fly an ordinary pitch,[23]

---

[15] *Intermit* is here equivalent to *remit*; that is, *avert*, or *turn back*.

[16] It is evident from the opening scene, that Shakespeare, even in dealing with classical subjects, laughed at the classic fear of putting the ludicrous and sublime into juxtaposition. After the low and farcical jests of the saucy cobbler, the eloquence of Marullus "springs upwards like a pyramid of fire."—CAMPBELL.

[17] The meaning is, "till your tears swell the river from the extreme low-water mark to the extreme high-water mark."

[18] *Whêr* for *whether*. The contraction occurs repeatedly in this play.—In *basest metal* Shakespeare probably had *lead* in his thought. So that the meaning is, that even these men, though as *dull* and *heavy* as lead, have yet the sense to be tongue-tied with shame at their conduct.

[19] These images were the busts and statues of Cæsar, ceremoniously decked with scarfs and badges in honour of his triumph.

[20] This festival, held in honour of Lupercus, the Roman Pan, fell on the 13th of February, which month was so named from Februus, a surname of the god. Lupercus was, primarily, the god of shepherds, said to have been so called because he kept off the wolves. His wife Luperca was the deified she-wolf that suckled Romulus. The festival, in its original idea, was meant for religious expiation and purification, February being at that time the last month of the year.

[21] "Cæsar's trophies" are the scarfs and badges mentioned in note 19; as appears in the next scene, where it is said that the Tribunes "are put to silence for pulling scarfs off Cæsar's images."

[22] The Poet often uses *vulgar* in its Latin sense of *common*. Here it means the common people.

Who else would soar above the view of men
And keep us all in servile fearfulness. [*Exeunt.*]

SCENE II.

The Same. A public Place.

[*Enter, in procession, with music,* CÆSAR; ANTONY, *for the course*; CALPURNIA, PORTIA, DECIUS BRUTUS, CICERO, BRUTUS, CASSIUS, *and* CASCA; *a great Crowd following, among them a Soothsayer.*]

CÆSAR. Calpurnia!
CASCA. Peace, ho! Cæsar speaks. [*Music ceases.*]
CÆSAR. Calpurnia!
CALPURNIA. Here, my lord.
CÆSAR. Stand you directly in Antonius's way,
    When he doth run his course.[24] Antonius!
ANTONY. Cæsar, my lord?
CÆSAR. Forget not, in your speed, Antonius,
    To touch Calpurnia; for our elders say,
    The barren, touched in this holy chase,
    Shake off their sterile curse.[25]
ANTONY. I shall remember:
    When Cæsar says 'do this,' it is perform'd.
CÆSAR. Set on; and leave no ceremony out. [*Music.*]
SOOTHSAYER. Cæsar!

---

[23] *Pitch* is here a technical term in falconry, and means the highest flight of a hawk or falcon.

[24] Marcus Antonius was at this time Consul, as Cæsar himself also was. Each Roman *gens* had its own priesthood, and also its peculiar religious rites. The priests of the Julian gens (so named from Iulus the son of Æneas) had lately been advanced to the same rank with those of the god Lupercus; and Antony was at this time at their head. It was probably as chief of the Julian Luperci that he officiated on this occasion in "the holy course." It may be well to add, here, that in old Roman society the *gens* was much the same as the Scottish *clan* in modern times; and that all the individuals, both male and female, of a given gens inherited what is called the gentilitial name; as Julius and Julia, Antonius and Antonia, Calpurnius and Calpurnia, Octavius and Octavia, Junius and Junia, Portius and Portia, Cassius and Cassia, Tullius and Tullia, &c.

[25] It was an old custom at these festivals for the priests, all naked except a girdle about the loins, to run through the streets of the city, waving in the hand a thong of goat's hide, and striking with it such women as offered themselves for the blow, in the belief that this would prevent or avert "the sterile curse."—Cæsar was at this time childless; his only daughter, Julia, married to Pompey the Great, having died some years before, upon the birth of her first child, who also died soon after. The Poet justly ascribes to Cæsar the natural desire of children to inherit his vast fame and honours; and this desire is aptly signified in the play, as such an ambition to be the founder of a royal or imperial line would be an additional motive for the conspiracy against him.

CÆSAR. Ha! who calls?
CASCA. Bid every noise be still: peace yet again!

[*Music ceases.*]

CÆSAR. Who is it in the press that calls on me?
I hear a tongue, shriller than all the music,
Cry *Cæsar!* Speak; Cæsar is turn'd to hear.
SOOTHSAYER. Beware the Ides of March.
CÆSAR. What man is that?
BRUTUS. A soothsayer bids you beware the Ides of March.[26]
CÆSAR. Set him before me; let me see his face.
CASSIUS. Fellow, come from the throng; look upon Cæsar.

[*The* SOOTHSAYER *comes forward.*]

CÆSAR. What say'st thou to me now? speak once again.
SOOTHSAYER. Beware the Ides of March.
CÆSAR. He is a dreamer; let us leave him.—Pass.

[*Sennet.*[27] *Exeunt all except* BRUTUS *and* CASSIUS.]

CASSIUS. Will you go see the order of the course?
BRUTUS. Not I.
CASSIUS. I pray you, do.
BRUTUS. I am not gamesome:[28] I do lack some part
Of that quick[29] spirit[30] that is in Antony.
Let me not hinder, Cassius, your desires;
I'll leave you.
CASSIUS. Brutus, I do observe you now of late:
I have not from your eyes that gentleness
And show of love as[31] I was wont to have:

---

[26] Coleridge has a remark on this line, which, whether true to the subject or not, is very characteristic of the writer: "If my ear does not deceive me, the metre of this line was meant to express that sort of mild philosophic contempt, characterizing Brutus even in his first casual speech." The metrical analysis of the line is, an Iamb, two Anapests, and two Iambs.

[27] *Sennet* is an old musical term occurring repeatedly in Shakespeare; of uncertain origin, but denoting a peculiar succession of notes on a trumpet, used, as here, to signal the march of a procession.

[28] *Gamesome* is *fond of sport*, or *sportively inclined.* Repeatedly so.

[29] *Quick* for *lively* or *animated.* So we have it in the phrases, "*quick* recreation," and "*quick* and merry words."

[30] *Spirit*, in Shakespeare, is often pronounced as one syllable, and sometimes spelt so,—*sprite, spright.*

[31] The demonstratives *this, that,* and *such,* and also the relatives *which, that,* and *as,* were often used indiscriminately. So a little later in this scene: "Under *these* hard

You bear too stubborn and too strange a hand
Over your friend that loves you.[32]
BRUTUS. Cassius,
  Be not deceived: if I have veil'd my look,
  I turn the trouble of my countenance
  Merely[33] upon myself. Vexed I am
  Of late with passions of some difference,[34]
  Conceptions only proper to myself,
  Which give some soil perhaps to my behaviors;[35]
  But let not therefore my good friends be grieved,—
  Among which number, Cassius, be you one—
  Nor construe[36] any further my neglect,
  Than that poor Brutus, with himself at war,
  Forgets the shows of love to other men.
CASSIUS. Then, Brutus, I have much mistook your passion;[37]
  By means whereof[38] this breast of mine hath buried
  Thoughts of great value, worthy cogitations.
  Tell me, good Brutus, can you see your face?
BRUTUS. No, Cassius; for the eye sees not itself,
  But by reflection, by some other thing.[39]
CASSIUS. 'Tis just:[40]
  And it is very much lamented, Brutus,
  That you have no such mirrors as will turn
  Your hidden worthiness into your eye,

---

conditions *as* this time is like to lay on us."

[32] This man, Caius Cassius Longinus, had married Junia, a sister of Brutus. Both had lately stood for the chief Praetorship of the city, and Brutus, through Cæsar's favour, had won it; though Cassius was at the same time elected one of the sixteen Praetors or judges of the city. This is said to have produced a coldness between Brutus and Cassius, so that they did not speak to each other, till this extraordinary flight of patriotism brought them together.

[33] *Merely,* here, is *altogether* or *entirely.* A frequent usage.

[34] That is, *conflicting* passions; such as his love to Cæsar personally, and his hatred of Cæsar's power in the State.

[35] "Which blemish or tarnish the lustre of my *manners.*" The Poet repeatedly uses the plural, *behaviours,* for the particular acts which make up what we call behaviour. And so of several other words.

[36] In Shakespeare, and, I think, in all other poetry, *construe* always has the accent on the first syllable. How or whence the present *vulgar* pronunciation of it came into use, I cannot say. The same, too, of *misconstrue,* which always has the accent on *con.*

[37] The Poet uses *mistook* and *mistaken* indiscriminately. He also sometimes uses *passion* for any feeling, sentiment, or emotion, whether painful or pleasant. So he has "more merry tears the *passion* of loud laughter never shed," and "free from gross *passion* or of mirth or anger."

[38] *Means* was sometimes used in the sense of *cause* or *reason. Whereof* refers to the preceding clause.

[39] By an image or "shadow" *reflected* from a mirror, or from water, or some polished surface.

[40] *'Tis just* is the same as our phrase, "That's so," or "Exactly so."

That you might see your shadow. I have heard,
Where many of the best respect[41] in Rome,—
Except immortal Cæsar, speaking of Brutus
And groaning underneath this age's yoke,
Have wish'd that noble Brutus had his eyes.

BRUTUS. Into what dangers would you lead me, Cassius,
That you would have me seek into myself
For that which is not in me?

CASSIUS. Therefore, good Brutus, be prepared to hear:
And since you know you cannot see yourself
So well as by reflection, I, your glass,
Will modestly discover to yourself
That of yourself which you yet know not of.
And be not jealous on[42] me, gentle Brutus:
Were I a common laugher, or did use
To stale[43] with ordinary oaths my love
To every new protester;[44] if you know
That I do fawn on men and hug them hard
And after scandal them, or if you know
That I profess myself in banqueting
To all the rout,[45] then hold me dangerous. [*Flourish, and shout.*]

BRUTUS. What means this shouting? I do fear, the people
Choose Cæsar for their king.

CASSIUS. Ay, do you fear it?
Then must I think you would not have it so.

BRUTUS. I would not, Cassius; yet I love him well.
But wherefore do you hold me here so long?
What is it that you would impart to me?
If it be aught toward the general good,
Set honour in one eye and death i' the other,
And I will look on both indifferently,
For let the gods so speed[46] me as I love

---

[41] The sense probably is, "I have *been present* where many of the *highest repute*, or held in the highest consideration." *Respect was* often used so.—"Except immortal Cassar!" is very emphatic, and intensely ironical.

[42] *On* and *of* were used indifferently in such cases. *Jealous*, also, for *doubtful* or *suspicious*. So a little further on: "That you do love me, I am nothing *jealous*."

[43] To *stale* a thing is to make it *common* or *cheap* by indiscriminate use. So in iv. 1, of this play: "Out of use, and *staled* by other men."—*Laugher*, if it be the right word, must mean *jester* or *buffoon*.

[44] To *protest* occurs frequently in the sense of to *profess*, to *declare*, or to *vow*. The passage is well explained by one in *Hamlet*, i. 3: "Do not dull thy palm with entertainment of each new-hatch'd, unfledged comrade."

[45] The order, according to the sense, is, "if you know that, in banqueting, I profess myself to all the rout."—To make his flattery work the better, Cassius here assures the "gentle Brutus" that he scorns to flatter, that he never speaks anything but austere truth, and that he is extremely select in his friendships.

The name of honour more than I fear death.
CASSIUS. I know that virtue to be in you, Brutus,
As well as I do know your outward favour.[47]
Well, honour is the subject of my story.
I cannot tell what you and other men
Think of this life; but, for my single self,
I had as lief[48] not be as live to be
In awe of such a thing as I myself.
I was born free as Cæsar; so were you:
We both have fed as well, and we can both
Endure the winter's cold as well as he:
For once, upon a raw and gusty day,
The troubled Tiber chafing with her shores,
Cæsar said to me *Darest thou, Cassius, now*
Leap in with me into this angry flood,
And swim to yonder point? Upon the word,
Accoutred as I was, I plunged in
And bade him follow; so indeed he did.
The torrent roar'd, and we did buffet it
With lusty sinews, throwing it aside
And stemming it with hearts of controversy;[49]
But ere we could arrive the point[50] proposed,
Cæsar cried *Help me, Cassius, or I sink!*
I, as Aeneas, our great ancestor,
Did from the flames of Troy upon his shoulder
The old Anchises bear, so from the waves of Tiber
Did I the tired Cæsar. And this man
Is now become a god, and Cassius is
A wretched creature and must bend his body,
If Cæsar carelessly but nod on him.
He had a fever when he was in Spain;[51]

---

[46] To *speed* for to *prosper* or *bless*; a frequent usage.

[47] *Favour* for *look, aspect,* or *appearance,* was very common.

[48] *Lief* or *lieve* is an old word for *glad* or *willing, gladly* or *willingly*; the opposite of *loth* or *loath*. Its original sense was about the same as *dear*.

[49] That is, with *contending* hearts; *heart* being put for *courage*. The Poet has many like expressions, as, "mind of love" for *loving mind*, "thieves of mercy" for *merciful thieves*, "time of scorn" for *scornful time*, &c.

[50] Shakespeare uses both *arrive* and *aspire* as transitive verbs, and in the sense of *reach* or *attain*. So Milton in *Paradise Lost*, ii. 409: "Ere he *arrive* the happy isle."

[51] *Fever* appears to have been used for *sickness* in general, as well as for what we call a fever. Cæsar had three several campaigns in Spain at different periods of his life, and the text does not show which of these Shakespeare had in mind. One passage in Plutarch would seem to infer that Cæsar was first taken with the epilepsy during his third campaign, which closed with the great battle of Munda, March 17, B.C. 45; but Plutarch elsewhere speaks of him as having the disease at an earlier period: "Concerning the constitution of his body, he was lean, white, and soft-skinned, and often subject to

And when the fit was on him, I did mark
How he did shake: 'tis true, this god did shake;
His coward lips did from their colour fly,[52]
And that same eye whose bend[53] doth awe the world
Did lose his[54] lustre: I did hear him groan:
Ay, and that tongue of his that bade the Romans
Mark him and write his speeches in their books,
Alas, it cried *Give me some drink, Titinius*,
As a sick girl. Ye gods, it doth amaze me
A man of such a feeble temper[55] should
So get the start of the majestic world
And bear the palm alone. [*Shout. Flourish.*]

BRUTUS. Another general shout!
I do believe that these applauses are
For some new honours that are heap'd on Cæsar.

CASSIUS. Why, man, he doth bestride the narrow world
Like a Colossus;[56] and we petty men
Walk under his huge legs and peep about
To find ourselves dishonourable graves.
Men at some time are masters of their fates:
The fault, dear Brutus, is not in our stars,[57]

---

headache, and otherwhile to the falling-sickness; the which took him the first time, as it is reported, in Corduba, a city of Spain; but yet therefore yielded not to the disease of his body, to make it a cloak to cherish him withal; but, contrarily, took the pains of war as a medicine to cure his sick body, fighting always with his disease, travelling continually, living soberly, and commonly lying abroad in the field."

[52] The image, very bold, somewhat forced, and not altogether happy, is of a cowardly soldier running away from his flag.

[53] *Bend* for *look*. The verb to *bend*, when used of the eyes, often has the sense of to *direct*.

[54] *His* for *its*, and referring to *eye*. *Its* was not then an accepted word, but was creeping into use; and the Poet has it several times. It does not once occur in the English Bible as first printed in 1611; and only twice, I think, in *Paradise Lost*, published in 1667.

[55] *Temper* for *constitution* or *temperament*.—"The lean and wrinkled Cassius" venting his spite at Cæsar, by ridiculing his liability to sickness and death, is charmingly characteristic. In fact, this mighty man, with all his electric energy of mind and will, was of a rather fragile and delicate make; and his countenance, as we have it in authentic busts, is almost a model of feminine beauty. Cicero, who did not love him at all, in one of his Letters applies to him a Greek word, the same that is used for *miracle* or *wonder* in the *New Testament*; the English of the passage being, "This miracle (monster?) is a thing of terrible energy, swiftness, diligence."

[56] Observe the force of *narrow* here; as if Cæsar were grown so enormously big that even the world seemed a little thing under him. Some while before this, the Senate had erected a bronze statue of Cæsar, standing on a globe, and inscribed to "Cæsar the Demigod"; which inscription, however, Cæsar had erased.—The original Colossus was a bronze statue a hundred and twenty feet high, set up astride a part of the harbour at Rhodes, so that ships passed "under its huge legs."

[57] Referring to the old astrological notion of planetary influence on the fortunes and characters of men. The Poet has many such allusions.

But in ourselves, that we are underlings.
Brutus and *Cæsar*: what should be in that *Cæsar*?[58]
Why should that name be sounded more than yours?
Write them together, yours is as fair a name;
Sound them, it doth become the mouth as well;
Weigh them, it is as heavy; conjure with 'em,
Brutus will start a spirit as soon as *Cæsar*.[59]
Now, in the names of all the gods at once,
Upon what meat doth this our Cæsar feed,
That he is grown so great? Age, thou art shamed!
Rome, thou hast lost the breed of noble bloods!
When went there by an age, since the great flood,[60]
But it was famed with more than with one man?
When could they say till now, that talk'd of Rome,
That her wide walls encompass'd but one man?
Now is it Rome indeed and room[61] enough,
When there is in it but one only man.
O, you and I have heard our fathers say,
There was a Brutus once[62] that would have brook'd
The eternal devil to keep his state[63] in Rome
As easily as a king.

BRUTUS. That you do love me, I am nothing jealous;
What you would work me to, I have some aim:[64]

---

[58] Meaning, "what *is* there in that word *Cæsar*?" The Poet often uses *should be* where we should use *is* or *can be*. So I have sometimes been asked, "What *might* your name be?"

[59] The allusion is to the old custom of muttering certain names, supposed to have in them "the might of magic spells," in raising or conjuring up spirits.—*Brutus* and *Casar* are here printed in Italic, to show that Cassius is referring to the magical power of the names, and not to the men.

[60] By this a Roman would of course mean Deucalion's flood.

[61] A play upon *Rome* and *room*, which appear to have been sounded more alike in Shakespeare's time than they are now.—In the next line, "but one only" is redundant or reduplicative, and means *but one*, or *only one*. Repeatedly so.

[62] Alluding to Lucius Junius Brutus, who bore a leading part in driving out the Tarquins, and in turning the Kingdom into a Republic. Afterwards, as Consul, he condemned his own sons to death for attempting to restore the Kingdom. The Marcus Junius Brutus of the play supposed himself to be lineally descended from him. His mother, Servilia, also derived her lineage from Servilius Ahala, who slew Spurius Mælius for aspiring to royalty. Merivale justly remarks that "the name of Brutus forced its possessor into prominence as soon as royalty began to be discussed."

[63] "Keep his state" may mean either preserve his dignity or set up his throne; *state* being repeatedly used for *throne*.—The Poet has *eternal* sereral times for *infernal*. Perhaps our Yankee phrases, "*tarnal* shame," "*tarnal* scamp," &c., are relics of this usage. It seems that the Puritans and Calvinists thought *infernal* too profane for godly mouths, and so transferred its sense to *eternal*.

[64] "Work me to" is *persuade* or *induce* me to.—*Aim* is *guess*. So the verb in *Romeo and Juliet*, i. 1: "I *aim'd* so near when I supposed you loved." And the Poet has it so in divers other places.

How I have thought of this and of these times,
I shall recount hereafter; for this present,
I would not, so with love I might entreat you,
Be any further moved. What you have said
I will consider; what you have to say
I will with patience hear, and find a time
Both meet to hear and answer such high things.
Till then, my noble friend, chew[65] upon this:
Brutus had rather be a villager
Than to repute himself[66] a son of Rome
Under these hard conditions as this time
Is like to lay upon us.

CASSIUS. I am glad that my weak words
Have struck but thus much show
Of fire[67] from Brutus.

BRUTUS. The games are done and Cæsar is returning.

CASSIUS. As they pass by, pluck Casca by the sleeve;
And he will, after his sour fashion, tell you
What hath proceeded[68] worthy note to-day.

[*Re-enter* CÆSAR *and his train.*]

BRUTUS. I will do so. But, look you, Cassius,
The angry spot doth glow on Cæsar's brow,
And all the rest look like a chidden train:
Calpurnia's cheek is pale; and Cicero
Looks with such ferret[69] and such fiery eyes
As we have seen him in the Capitol,
Being cross'd in conference by some senators.

CASSIUS. Casca will tell us what the matter is.

CÆSAR. Antonius!

ANTONY. Cæsar?

CÆSAR. Let me have men about me that are fat;

---

[65] To *chew* is, literally, to *ruminate*; that is, *reflect* or *meditate*. So in *As You Like It*, iv. 3: "*Chewing the cud* of sweet and bitter fancy."

[66] An irregular construction, but common in the Poet's time. So Bacon in his essay *Of Friendship*: "A man were better relate himself to a statue or picture than *to* suffer his thoughts to pass in smother."

[67] Referring to the use of steel and flint in starting a fire. So, in *Troilus and Cressida*, iii. 3, Thersites says of Ajax's wit, "It lies as coldly in him as fire in a flint, which will not show without knocking."

[68] That is, hath *happened* or *come to pass*. Repeatedly so.

[69] The ferret is a very ferocious little animal of the weasel kind, noted for its fire-red eyes.—The angry spot on Cæsar's brow, Calpurnia's pale cheek, and Cicero spouting fire from his eyes as when kindled by opposition in the Senate, make an exceedingly vivid picture.

Sleek-headed men and such as sleep o' nights:
Yond Cassius has a lean and hungry look;
He thinks too much:[70] such men are dangerous.
ANTONY. Fear him not, Cæsar; he's not dangerous;
He is a noble Roman and well given.[71]
CÆSAR. Would he were fatter! But I fear him not:
Yet if my name were liable to fear,
I do not know the man I should avoid
So soon as that spare Cassius. He reads much;
He is a great observer and he looks
Quite through the deeds of men: he loves no plays,[72]
As thou dost, Antony; he hears no music:[73]
Seldom he smiles, and smiles in such a sort
As if he mock'd himself and scorn'd his spirit
That could be moved to smile at any thing.
Such men as he be never at heart's ease
Whiles they behold a greater than themselves,
And therefore are they very dangerous.
I rather tell thee what is to be fear'd
Than what I fear; for always I am Cæsar.
Come on my right hand, for this ear is deaf,[74]
And tell me truly what thou think'st of him.

---

[70] So in North's Plutarch, *Life of Julius Cæsar:* "When Cæsar's friends complained unto him of Antonius and Dolabella, that they intended some mischief towards him, he answered them, As for those fat men, and smooth-combed heads, I never reckon of them; but these pale-visaged and carrion-lean people, I fear them most; meaning Brutus and Cassius."

[71] *Well given* is *well disposed.* So in North's Plutarch: "If there were any noble attempt done in all this conspiracy, they refer it wholly unto Brutus; and all the cruel and violent acts unto Cassius, who was Brutus's familiar friend, but not so *well given* and conditioned as he."

[72] This is from Plutarch's *Life of Antonius:* "In his house they did nothing but feast, dance, and masque; and himself passed away the time in hearing of foolish plays, and in marrying these players, tumblers, jesters, and such sort of people."

[73] The power of music is repeatedly celebrated by Shakespeare, and sometimes in strains that approximate the classical hyperboles about Orpheus, Amphion, and Arion. What is here said of Cassius has an apt commentary in *The Merchant of Venice,* v. 1:

> The man that hath no music in himself,
> Nor is not moved with concord of sweet sounds,
> Is fit for treasons, stratagems, and spoils;
> The motions of his spirit are dull as night,
> And his affections dark as Erebus:
> Let no such man be trusted.

[74] This is one of the little touches of invention that so often impart a fact-like vividness to the Poet's scenes; like that remarked in note **Error! Bookmark not defined.**.

[*Exeunt* CÆSAR *and all his train, except* CASCA.]

CASCA. You pull'd me by the cloak; would you speak with me?
BRUTUS. Ay, Casca; tell us what hath chanced to-day,
That Cæsar looks so sad.[75]
CASCA. Why, you were with him, were you not?
BRUTUS. I should not then ask Casca what had chanced.
CASCA. Why, there was a crown offered him: and being offered him,
he put it by with the back of his hand, thus; and then the people fell
a-shouting.
BRUTUS. What was the second noise for?
CASCA. Why, for that too.
CASSIUS. They shouted thrice: what was the last cry for?
CASCA. Why, for that too.
BRUTUS. Was the crown offered him thrice?
CASCA. Ay, marry,[76] was't, and he put it by thrice, every time gentler
than other, and at every putting-by mine honest neighbours
shouted.
CASSIUS. Who offered him the crown?
CASCA. Why, Antony.
BRUTUS. Tell us the manner of it, gentle Casca.
CASCA. I can as well be hanged as tell the manner of it: it was mere
foolery; I did not mark it. I saw Mark Antony offer him a crown;—
yet 'twas not a crown neither, 'twas one of these coronets;—and,
as I told you, he put it by once: but, for all that, to my thinking, he
would fain[77] have had it. Then he offered it to him again; then he
put it by again: but, to my thinking, he was very loath to lay his
fingers off it. And then he offered it the third time; he put it the
third time by: and still as he refused it, the rabblement hooted and
clapped their chapped hands and threw up their sweaty night-caps
and uttered such a deal of stinking breath because Cæsar refused
the crown that it had almost choked Cæsar; for he swooned and fell
down at it: and for mine own part, I durst not laugh, for fear of
opening my lips and receiving the bad air.[78]

---

[75] *Sad* in its old sense of *grave* or *serious*, probably. A frequent usage. So, in *Romeo and Juliet*, i. 1, Benvolio says, "Tell me in *sadness*, who 'tis that you love"; and Romeo replies, "In *sadness*, cousin, I do love a woman."

[76] From an old custom of appealing to the Virgin Mary, *marry* grew into common use as an intensive; like *verily, indeed, to be sure*. So the Latin often has *heracle* and *edepol*; the latter from swearing by Castor and Pollux.

[77] *Fain* is glad or gladly; much used in the Poet's time. So in St. Luke, xv. 16: "He would *fain* have filled his belly with the husks," &c.

[78] Cæsar sat to behold that sport upon the pulpit for orations, in a chain of gold, apparelled in triumphant manner. Antonius, who was Consul at that time, was one of them that ran this holy course. So when he came into the market-place the people made a lane for him to run at liberty, and he came to Cæsar, and presented him a diadem

CASSIUS. But, soft![79] I pray you: what, did Cæsar swoon?
CASCA. He fell down in the market-place, and foamed at mouth, and
    was speechless.
BRUTUS. 'Tis very like: he hath the failing sickness.
CASSIUS. No, Cæsar hath it not; but you and I,
And honest Casca, we have the falling sickness.[80]
CASCA. I know not what you mean by that; but, I am sure, Cæsar fell
    down. If the tag-rag people did not clap him and hiss him,
    according as he pleased and displeased them, as they use to do the
    players in the theatre, I am no true man.[81]
BRUTUS. What said he when he came unto himself?
CASCA. Marry, before he fell down, when he perceived the common
    herd was glad he refused the crown, he plucked me ope his
    doublet,[82] and offered them his throat to cut: an I had been a man
    of any occupation,[83] if I would not have taken him at a word, I
    would I might go to hell among the rogues. And so he fell. When
    he came to himself again, he said, If he had done or said any thing
    amiss, he desired their worships to think it was his infirmity.[84]
    Three or four wenches, where I stood, cried *Alas, good soul!* and
    forgave him with all their hearts: but there's no heed to be taken of

---

wreathed about with laurel. Whereupon there rose a certain cry of rejoicing, not very
great, done only by a few appointed for the purpose. But when Cæsar refused the diadem,
then all the people together made an outcry of joy. Then Antonius offering it him again,
there was a second shout of joy, but yet of a few. But when Cæsar refused it again the
second time, then all the whole people shouted. Cæsar having made this proof, found that
the people did not like of it, and thereupon rose out of his chair, and commanded the
crown to be carried unto Jupiter in the Capitol.—PLUTARCH.

    [79] *Soft!* was much used as an exclamation for arresting or retarding the speed of a
person or thing; meaning about the same as *hold! stay! or not too fast!* So in *Othello*, v. 2:
"*Soft* you! a word or two before you go."

    [80] Meaning the disease of "standing prostrate" before Cæsar. *Falling sickness* or
falling-evil was the English name for epilepsy. Cæsar was subject to it, especially in his
later years, as Napoleon also is said to have been. See page 24, note 51.

    [81] "*True* man" is *honest* man. Often used in that sense, but especially as opposed to
thief. So in *Cymbeline*, ii. 3: "'Tis gold which makes the true man kill'd, and saves the
thief; nay, sometimes hangs both thief and true man." Also in *Venus and Adonis*: "Rich
preys make true men thieves."

    [82] *Doublet* was the common English name of a man's upper outward garment.—In
this clause, *me* is simply redundant; as in Falstaff's speech in praise of sack: "It ascends
me into the brain; dries *me* there all the foolish and dull and crudy vapours which environ
it."

    [83] "A man of occupation" probably means not only a mechanic or user of cutting-
tools, but also a man of business and of action, as distinguished from a gentleman of
leisure, or an idler.—*An*, in this clause, is an old equivalent for *if.* Often used thus by the
Poet.

    [84] Thereupon Cæsar rising departed home to his house; and, tearing open his
doublet-collar, making his neck bear, he cried out aloud to his friends, that his throat was
ready to offer to any man that would come and cut it. Notwithstanding it is reported that,
afterwards, to excuse his folly, he imputed it to his disease, saying that their wits are not
perfect which have this disease of the falling-evil.—PLUTARCH.

them; if Cæsar had stabbed their mothers, they would have done no less.

BRUTUS. And after that, he came, thus sad, away?

CASCA. Ay.

CASSIUS. Did Cicero say any thing?

CASCA. Ay, he spoke Greek.

CASSIUS. To what effect?

CASCA. Nay, an I tell you that, Ill ne'er look you i' the face again: but those that understood him smiled at one another and shook their heads; but, for mine own part, it was Greek to me.[85] I could tell you more news too: Marellus and Flavius, for pulling scarves off Cæsar's images, are put to silence. Fare you well. There was more foolery yet, if I could remember it.

CASSIUS. Will you sup with me to-night, Casca?

CASCA. No, I am promised forth.[86]

CASSIUS. Will you dine with me to-morrow?

CASCA. Ay, if I be alive and your mind hold and your dinner worth the eating.

CASSIUS. Good: I will expect you.

CASCA. Do so. Farewell, both. [*Exit.*]

BRUTUS. What a blunt[87] fellow is this grown to be!
He was quick mettle when he went to school.

CASSIUS. So is he now in execution
Of any bold or noble enterprise,
However he puts on this tardy form.[88]
This rudeness is a sauce to his good wit,
Which gives men stomach to digest his words
With better appetite.

BRUTUS. And so it is. For this time I will leave you:
To-morrow, if you please to speak with me,
I will come home to you; or, if you will,
Come home to me, and I will wait for you.

CASSIUS. I will do so: till then, think of the world.

---

[85] A charming invention. Cicero had a long, sharp, agile tongue, and was mighty fond of using it; and nothing was more natural, supposing him to have been present, than that he should snap off some keen sententious sayings; prudently veiling them however in a foreign language from all but those who might safely understand them. In fact, it was his incontinence of sarcasm that finally enraged Antony to the killing of him.

[86] Shakespeare *has forth* very often with the sense of *out* or *abroad.*

[87] *Blunt* here means, apparently, *dull* or *slow*; alluding to the "tardy form" Casca has just "put on" in winding so long about the matter before coming to the point.—"He was quick mettle" means, He was of a *lively spirit. Mettlesome* is still used of spirited horses.

[88] *However* for *although* or *notwithstanding.* Often so.—"Tardy" form" is form of *tardiness.* So the Poet has *shady stealth* for *stealing shadow,* and "*negligent* danger" for danger *from negligence.*

[*Exit* BRUTUS.]

Well, Brutus, thou art noble; yet, I see,
Thy honourable metal may be wrought
From that it is disposed:[89] therefore 'tis meet
That noble minds keep ever with their likes;
For who so firm that cannot be seduced?
Cæsar doth bear me hard,[90] but he loves Brutus:
If I were Brutus now and he were Cassius,
He should not humour me.[91] I will this night,
In several hands,[92] in at his windows throw,
As if they came from several citizens,
Writings all tending to the great opinion
That Rome holds of his name; wherein obscurely
Cæsar's ambition shall be glanced at:
And after this let Cæsar seat him sure;
For we will shake him, or worse days endure.[93] [*Exit.*]

SCENE III.

The Same. A Street.

[*Thunder and lightning. Enter, from opposite sides,* CASCA, *with
his sword drawn, and* CICERO.]

---

[89] Wrought from *what*, or from that *which* it is disposed *to*. The Poet has divers instances of prepositions thus omitted.—Cassius is here chuckling over the effect his talk has had upon Brutus. He evidently regards Brutus as a noble putty-head, and goes on to take order for moulding him accordingly.

[90] The phrase to *bear one hard* occurs three times in this play, but nowhere else in Shakespeare. It seems to have been borrowed from horsemanship, and to mean *carries a tight rein*, or *reins hard*, like one who *distrusts* his horse. So before: "You bear too stubborn and too strange a hand over your friend that loves you"; that is, "You hold me too hard on the bit, like a strange rider, who is doubtful of his steed, and not like one who confides in his faithful horse, and so rides him with an easy rein."—For this note I am indebted to Mr. Joseph Crosby.

[91] To *humour* a man, as the word is here used, is to turn and wind and manage him by watching his moods and crotchets, and touching him accordingly. It is somewhat in doubt whether the last *he* refers to Brutus or to Cæsar. If to Brutus, the meaning of course is, "he should not play upon my humours and fancies as I do upon his." And this sense is, I think, fairly required by the context. For the whole speech is occupied with the speaker's success in cajoling Brutus, and with plans for cajoling and shaping him still further.

[92] *Hands* for *handwritings*, of course. The Poet has it repeatedly so.

[93] "We will either shake him, or endure worse days in suffering the consequences of our attempt."—The Poet makes Cassius overflow with intense personal spite against Cæsar. This is in accordance with what he read in Plutarch: "Cassius, being a choleric man, and hating Cæsar privately more than he did the tyranny openly, incensed Brutus against him. It is also reported that Brutus could evil away with the tyranny, and that Cassius hated the tyrant." Of course *tyranny* as here used means *royalty*.

CICERO. Good even, Casca: brought you Cæsar home?[94]
  Why are you breathless? and why stare you so?
CASCA. Are not you moved, when all the sway of earth
  Shakes like a thing unfirm?[95] O Cicero,
  I have seen tempests, when the scolding winds
  Have rived the knotty oaks, and I have seen
  The ambitious ocean swell and rage and foam,
  To be exalted with the threatening clouds:[96]
  But never till to-night, never till now,
  Did I go through a tempest dropping fire.
  Either there is a civil strife in heaven,
  Or else the world, too saucy with the gods,
  Incenses them to send destruction.[97]
CICERO. Why, saw you any thing more[98] wonderful?
CASCA. A common slave—you know him well by sight[99]—
  Held up his left hand, which did flame and burn
  Like twenty torches join'd, and yet his hand,
  Not sensible[100] of fire, remain'd unscorch'd.
  Besides—I ha' not since put up my sword—
  Against the Capitol I met a lion,
  Who glared upon me, and went surly by,
  Without annoying me: and there were drawn
  Upon a heap[101] a hundred ghastly women,
  Transformed with their fear; who swore they saw
  Men all in fire walk up and down the streets.
  And yesterday the bird of night[102] did sit
  Even at noon-day upon the market-place,
  Hooting and shrieking. When these prodigies

---

[94] To *bring* for to *escort* or *go along with* was very common.

[95] *Sway* for *constitution* or *order*, probably. In such a raging of the elements, it seems as if the whole world were going to pieces, or as if the Earth's steadfastness were growing *unfirm*, that is, unsteady.

[96] *So as*, or *insomuch as* to be exalted with the threatening clouds. The Poet often uses the infinitive mood thus.

[97] Either the gods are fighting among themselves, or else they are making war on the world for being too saucy with them.

[98] *More* is here equivalent to *else*: "Saw you any thing more *that was* wonderful?"

[99] "You would *recognize* him as a common slave, from his looks."

[100] *Sensible*, here, is *sensitive*, or having sensation. Repeatedly so.

[101] That is, drawn *together in a crowd.*

[102] The old Roman horror of this bird is well shown in a passage of Holland's Pliny, as quoted in the Clarendon edition: "The screechowl betokeneth always some heavy news, and is most execrable in the presages of public affairs. In sum, he is the very monster of the night. There fortuned one of them to enter the very sanctuary of the Capitol, in that year when Sextus Papellio Ister and Lucius Pedanius were Consuls; whereupon, at the Nones of March, the city of Rome that year made general processions, to appease the wrath of the gods, and was solemnly purged by sacrifices."

Do so conjointly meet,[103] let not men say
These are their reasons; they are natural;[104]
For, I believe, they are portentous things
Unto the climate[105] that they point upon.

CICERO. Indeed, it is a strange-disposed time:
But men may construe things after their fashion,
Clean[106] from the purpose of the things themselves.
Come Cæsar to the Capitol to-morrow?

CASCA. He doth; for he did bid Antonius
Send word to you he would be there to-morrow.

CICERO. Good night then, Casca: this disturbed sky
Is not to walk in.

CASCA. Farewell, Cicero. [*Exit* CICERO.]

[*Enter* CASSIUS.]

CASSIUS. Who's there?

CASCA. A Roman.

CASSIUS. Casca, by your voice.

CASCA. Your ear is good. Cassius, what night is this![107]

CASSIUS. A very pleasing night to honest men.

CASCA. Who ever knew the heavens menace so?

CASSIUS. Those that have known the earth so full of faults.

---

[103] Certainly destiny may easier be foreseen than avoided, considering the strange and wonderful signs that were said to be seen before Cæsar's death. For, touching the fires in the element, and spirits running up and down in the night, and also the solitary birds to be seen at noondays sitting in the great market-place, are not all these signs perhaps worth the noting, in such a wonderful chance as happened? But Strabo the philosopher writeth, that divers men were seen going up and down in fire, and furthermore, that there was a slave of the soldiers that did cast a marvellous burning flame out of his hand, insomuch as they that saw it thought he had been burnt; but when the fire was out, it was found he had no hurt. Cæsar self also, doing sacrifice unto the gods, found that one of the beasts which was sacrificed had no heart: and that was a strange thing in nature, how a beast could live without a heart.—PLUTARCH.

[104] The language is obscure, but the meaning probably is, "These things *have* their reasons; they proceed from natural causes." Casca refers to the doctrine of the Epicureans, who were slow to believe that such elemental pranks had any moral significance in them, or that moral causes had anything to do with them; and held that the reasons of them were to be sought for in the simple working of natural laws and forces. The text has a good comment in *All's Well that Ends Well*, ii. 3: "They say miracles are past; and we have our philosophical persons, to make modern and familiar, things supernatural and causeless. Hence it is that we make trifles of terrors; ensconcing ourselves into seeming knowledge, when we should submit ourselves to an unknown fear."

[105] *Climate* for *region* or *country*. In *Hamlet* we have *climature* with the same meaning. Also "Christian *climate*" in *Richard the Second*, iv. 1.

[106] *Clean*, here, is *altogether, entirely*, or *quite*. Repeatedly so.

[107] We should say, "What *a* night is this!" In such exclamative phrases, as also in some others, the Poet omits the article when his verse wants it so.

For my part, I have walk'd about the streets,
Submitting me unto the perilous night,
And, thus unbraced,[108] Casca, as you see,
Have bared my bosom to the thunder-stone:[109]
And when the cross[110] blue lightning seem'd to open
The breast of heaven, I did present myself
Even in the aim and very flash of it.
CASCA. But wherefore did you so much tempt the heavens?
It is the part of men to fear and tremble,
When the most mighty gods by tokens send
Such dreadful heralds to astonish us.
CASSIUS. You are dull, Casca, and those sparks of life
That should be in a Roman you do want,
Or else you use not. You look pale and gaze
And put on fear and cast yourself in wonder,[111]
To see the strange impatience of the heavens:
But if you would consider the true cause
Why all these fires, why all these gliding ghosts,
Why birds and beasts from quality and kind;[112]
Why old men fool and children calculate;—
Why all these things change from their ordinance
Their natures and preformed faculties
To monstrous quality;[113]—why, you shall find
That heaven hath infused them with these spirits,
To make them instruments of fear and warning
Unto some monstrous state.[114] Now could I, Casca,
Name to thee a man most like this dreadful night,
That thunders, lightens, opens graves, and roars
As doth the lion in the Capitol,[115]

---

[108] *Unbuttoned.* Shakespeare gives the Romans his own dressing-gear.

[109] *Thunder-stone* is the old word for *thunder-bolt.*

[110] *Cross* for the *zigzag path* of lightning. So in *King Lear*, iv. 7: "Was this a face to stand in the most terrible and nimble stroke of quick, *cross* lightning?"

[111] That is, *put on a look* or *expression* of wonder. So in *Much Ado*, iv. 1: "I am so *attired in wonder*, I know not what to say."

[112] *Quality* is *office* or *calling*. Often so. *Kind* is *nature*. Also frequent. So in *Antony and Cleopatra*, last scene: "The worm will do his kind"; that is, will do as its *nature* is or prompts. The same in the old proverb, "The cat will after kind."—To make sense of the line, some word must be understood; probably *change*, from the second line below.

[113] The grammar of this passage is rather confused, yet the meaning is clear enough; the general idea being that of elements and animals, and even of old men and children, acting in a manner out of or against their nature; or changing their natures and original faculties from the course, in which they were ordained to move, to monstrous or unnatural modes of action.

[114] That is, some prodigious or abnormal condition of things. Elsewhere the Poet has "enormous state," with the same meaning.

[115] This reads as if a lion were kept in the Capitol to roar for them. But the meaning is that Cæsar roars in the Capitol, like a lion. Perhaps Cassius has the idea of Cæsar's

A man no mightier than thyself or me
In personal action, yet prodigious grown
And fearful, as these strange eruptions are.
CASCA. 'Tis Cæsar that you mean; is it not, Cassius?
CASSIUS. Let it be who it is,[116] for Romans now
Have thews[117] and limbs like to their ancestors;
But, woe the while! our fathers' minds are dead,
And we are govern'd with[118] our mothers' spirits;
Our yoke and sufferance show us womanish.
CASCA. Indeed, they say the senators tomorrow
Mean to establish Cæsar as a king;
And he shall wear his crown by sea and land,
In every place, save here in Italy.
CASSIUS. [*Drawing a dagger.*] I know where I will wear this dagger
then;
Cassius from bondage will deliver Cassius:
Therein, ye gods, you make the weak most strong;
Therein, ye gods, you tyrants do defeat:
Nor stony tower, nor walls of beaten brass,
Nor airless dungeon, nor strong links of iron,
Can be retentive to the strength of spirit;[119]
But life, being weary of these worldly bars,
Never lacks power to dismiss itself.
If I know this, know all the world besides,
That part of tyranny that I do bear
I can shake off at pleasure. [*Thunder still.*]
CASCA. So can I:
So every bondman in his own hand bears
The power to cancel his captivity.
CASSIUS. And why should Cæsar be a tyrant then?
Poor man! I know he would not be a wolf,
But that he sees the Romans are but sheep:
He were no lion, were not Romans hinds.
Those that with haste will make a mighty fire
Begin it with weak straws:[120] what trash is Rome,

---

claiming or aspiring to be among men what the lion is among beasts.

[116] Meaning, probably, "no matter who it is"; as the Clarendon notes.

[117] *Thews* for *sinews* or *muscles.* Always so in Shakespeare.

[118] Present usage would say "governed *by.*" But Shakespeare very often uses *with* to denote the agent of a passive verb. So afterwards in this play: "Here is himself, marr'd, as you see, *with* traitors."

[119] Can *retain, hold in,* or *repress* man's energy of soul.

[120] The idea seems to be that, as men start a huge fire with worthless straws or shavings, so Cæsar is using the degenerate Romans of the time, to set the whole world a-blaze with his own glory. Cassius's enthusiastic hatred of "the mightiest Julius" is irresistibly delightful. For "a good hater" is the next best thing to a true friend; and

What rubbish and what offal, when it serves
For the base matter to illuminate
So vile a thing as Cæsar!¹²¹ But, O grief,
Where hast thou led me? I perhaps speak this
Before a willing bondman; then I know
My answer must be made. But I am arm'd,
And dangers are to me indifferent.¹²²
CASCA. You speak to Casca, and to such a man
That is no fleering tell-tale.¹²³ Hold, my hand:
Be factious for redress of all these griefs;¹²⁴
And I will set this foot of mine as far
As who goes farthest.

[*They join hands.*]

CASSIUS. There's a bargain made.
Now know you, Casca, I have moved already
Some certain of the noblest-minded Romans
To undergo¹²⁵ with me an enterprise
Of honourable-dangerous consequence;
And I do know, by this,¹²⁶ they stay for me
In Pompey's porch: for now, this fearful night,
There is no stir or walking in the streets;
And the complexion of the element
In favour'd like¹²⁷ the work we have in hand,

Cassius's honest gushing malice is far better than Brutus's stabbing sentimentalism.

[121] To shed splendour upon him, or to make a light for him to shine by.

[122] The meaning is, "Perhaps you will go and blab to Cæsar all I have said about him; and then he will call me to account for it. Very well; go tell him; and let him do his worst: I care not."

[123] *Fleering* unites the two senses of flattering and *mocking*, and so is just the right epithet for a tell-tale, who flatters you into saying that of another which you ought not to say, and then mocks you by going to that other and telling what you have said.—The meaning of the next clause is, "Hold, *here is* my hand"; as men clasp hands in sealing a bargain.

[124] *Be factious* is, probably, *form a party* or *faction.* Or it may mean "Be *active*"; the literal meaning of *factious.*—Here, as often, *griefs* is put for *grievances*; that which *causes* griefs.

[125] *Undergo* for *undertake.* So in *Henry the Fourth, Part 2,* i. 3: "How able such a work to *undergo.*" And in several other places.

[126] *By this* for by this *time.* So in various instances.—Pompey's porch was a spacious adjunct to the huge theatre that Pompey had built in the Campus Martius, outside of the city proper; and where, as Plutarch says, "was set up an image of Pompey," which the city had made and consecrated in honour of him." There it was, in fact, that the stabbing took place, though Shakespeare transfers this to the Capitol.

[127] Is *featured*, has the same *aspect* or *countenance.* Shakespeare often *uses favour* in this sense. In the Poet's time, it was much in fashion to use *element* for *sky.* We have a ludicrous instance of this from Falstaff, in *Henry the Fourth, Part 2,* iv. 3: "If you do not all show like gilt two-pences to me, and I, in the clear sky of fame, o'ershine you as much

Most bloody, fiery, and most terrible.
CASCA. Stand close[128] awhile, for here comes one in haste.
CASSIUS. 'Tis Cinna; I do know him by his gait;
He is a friend.—

[*Enter* CINNA.]

Cinna, where haste you so?
CINNA. To find out you. Who's that? Metellus Cimber?
CASSIUS. No, it is Casca; one incorporate[129]
To our attempts. Am I not stay'd for, Cinna?
CINNA. I am glad on't. What a fearful night is this!
There's two or three of us have seen strange sights.
CASSIUS. Am I not stay'd for? tell me.
CINNA. Yes, you are.
O Cassius, if you could
But win the noble Brutus to our party—
CASSIUS. Be you content: good Cinna, take this paper,
And look you lay it in the prætor's chair,
Where Brutus may but find it; and throw this
In at his window; set this up with wax
Upon old Brutus' statue: all this done,
Repair to Pompey's porch, where you shall find us.
Is Decius Brutus and Trebonius there?
CINNA. All but Metellus Cimber; and he's gone
To seek you at your house. Well, I will hie,[130]
And so bestow these papers as you bade me.
CASSIUS. That done, repair to Pompey's theatre.

[*Exit* CINNA.]

Come, Casca, you and I will yet ere day
See Brutus at his house: three parts of him
Is[131] ours already, and the man entire
Upon the next encounter yields him ours.
CASCA. O, he sits high in all the people's hearts:
And that which would appear offence in us,
His countenance, like richest alchemy,[132]

---

as the full Moon doth the cinders of the *element*, which show like pins' heads to her,
believe not the word of a noble."
    [128] *Close* is *secret* or *in concealment.* A frequent usage.
    [129] *Incorporate* is *closely united,* like the several parts of the body.
    [130] *Hie* is *hasten.* So in *Hamlet,* i. 1: "Th' extravagant and erring spirit *hies* to his
confine." And in many other places.
    [131] Such combinations as *parts* and *is* were not then bad grammar.

Will change to virtue and to worthiness.
CASSIUS. Him and his worth and our great need of him
  You have right well conceited.[133] Let us go,
  For it is after midnight; and ere day
  We will awake him and be sure of him. [*Exeunt.*]

ACT II.

SCENE I.

Rome. BRUTUS's *Orchard.*[134]

[*Enter* BRUTUS.]

BRUTUS. What, Lucius, ho!
  I cannot, by the progress of the stars,
  Give guess how near to day. Lucius, I say!
  I would it were my fault to sleep so soundly.
  When, Lucius, when![135] awake, I say! what, Lucius!

[*Enter* LUCIUS.]

LUCIUS. Call'd you, my lord?
BRUTUS. Get me a taper in my study, Lucius:
  When it is lighted, come and call me here.
LUCIUS. I will, my lord. [*Exit.*]
BRUTUS. It must be by his death:[136] and for my part,
  I know no personal cause to spurn at him,
  But for the general.[137] He would be crown'd:
  How that might change his nature, there's the question.
  It is the bright day that brings forth the adder;[138]
  And that craves wary walking. Crown him?—that;—
  And then, I grant, we put a sting in him,
  That at his will he may do danger with.[139]

---

[132] Alchemy is the old *ideal* art of turning base metals into gold.

[133] *Conceited* is *conceived, understood,* or *apprehended.*

[134] *Orchard* and *garden* were synonymous. *In Romeo and Juliet,* Capulet's *garden* is twice called *orchard.*

[135] *When*! was sometimes used as an exclamation of impatience.

[136] Brutus has been casting about on all sides to find some other means to prevent Cæsar's being king, and here gives it up that this can be done only by killing him. Thus the speech opens in just the right way to throw us back upon his antecedent meditations.

[137] The *public cause.* This use of *general* was common.

[138] The Poet is apt to be right in his observation of Nature. In a bright warm day the snakes come out to bask in the sun. And the idea is, that the sunshine of royalty will kindle the serpent in Cæsar.

The abuse of greatness is, when it disjoins
Remorse from power: and, to speak truth of Cæsar,
I have not known when his affections sway'd
More than his reason.[140] But 'tis a common proof,[141]
That lowliness is young ambition's ladder,
Whereto the climber-upward turns his face;
But when he once attains the upmost round.
He then unto the ladder turns his back,
Looks in the clouds, scorning the base degrees[142]
By which he did ascend. So Cæsar may.
Then, lest he may, prevent. And, since the quarrel[143]
Will bear no colour for the thing he is,
Fashion it thus; that what he is, augmented,
Would run to these and these extremities:[144]
And therefore think him as a serpent's egg
Which, hatch'd, would, as his kind, grow mischievous,
And kill him in the shell.

[*Re-enter* LUCIUS.]

LUCIUS. The taper burneth in your closet, sir.
Searching the window for a flint, I found [*Gives him a paper.*]
This paper, thus seal'd up; and, I am sure,
It did not lie there when I went to bed.
BRUTUS. Get you to bed again; it is not day.

---

[139] That is, do *mischief* with, and so or *prove dangerous.*

[140] Some obscurity here, owing to the use of certain words in uncommon senses. *Remorse,* in Shakespeare, commonly means *pity* or *compassion*: here it means *conscience,* or *conscientiousness.* So in *Othello,* iii. 3: "Let him command, and to obey shall be in me *remorse,* what bloody work soe'er." The possession of dictatorial power is apt to stifle or sear the conscience, so as to make a man literally remorseless. *Affections,* again, here stands for *passions,* as in several other instances. Finally, *reason* is here used in the same sense as *remorse.* So the context clearly points out; and the conscience is, in a philosophical sense, the *moral* reason.

[141] *Proof* for *fact,* or the thing *proved.* The Poet has it repeatedly so.

[142] *Base degrees* is *lower steps*; *degree* being used in its primitive sense, and for the rounds of the ladder. Elsewhere the Poet has *base* for *lower.*

[143] *Quarrel* for *cause.* So in the 35th Psalm of *The Psalter*: "Stand up to judge my *quarrel*; avenge Thou my *cause.*"

[144] Something of obscurity again. But the meaning is, "Since we have no *show* or *pretext* of a cause, no assignable or apparent ground of complaint, against Cæsar, in what he is, or in any thing he has yet done, let us assume that the further addition of a crown will quite upset his nature, and metamorphose him into a serpent." The strain of casuistry used in this speech is very remarkable. Coleridge found it perplexing. Upon the supposal that Shakespeare meant Brutus for a wise and good man, the speech seems to me utterly unintelligible. But the Poet, I think, must have regarded him simply as a well-meaning, but conceited and shallow idealist; and such men are always cheating and puffing themselves with the thinnest of sophisms; feeding on air, and conceiving themselves inspired; or "mistaking the giddiness of the head for the illumination of the Spirit."

Is not to-morrow, boy, the Ides of March?
LUCIUS. I know not, sir.
BRUTUS. Look in the calendar, and bring me word.
LUCIUS. I will, sir. [*Exit.*]
BRUTUS. The exhalations,[145] whizzing in the air
Give so much light that I may read by them.

[*Opens the letter and reads.*]

Brutus, thou sleep'st: awake, and see thyself.
Shall Rome, & c. Speak, strike, redress!—
Brutus, thou sleep'st: awake!—
Such instigations have been often dropp'd
Where I have took them up.[146]
Shall Rome, & c. Thus must I piece it out:
Shall Rome stand under one man's awe? What, Rome?
My ancestors did from the streets of Rome
The Tarquin drive, when he was call'd a king.
Speak, strike, redress!—Am I entreated
To speak and strike? O Rome, I make thee promise:
If the redress will follow, thou receivest
Thy full petition at the hand of Brutus!

[*Re-enter LUCIUS.*]

LUCIUS. Sir, March is wasted fourteen days. [*Knocking within.*]
BRUTUS. 'Tis good. Go to the gate; somebody knocks.

[*Exit LUCIUS.*]

Since Cassius first did whet me against Cæsar,
I have not slept.
Between the acting of a dreadful thing

---

[145] *Exhalations* for *meteors*, or *metoric lights*; referring to the flashes of lightning. In Plutarch's *Opinions of Philosophers*, as translated by Holland, we have the following: "Aristotle supposeth that all these *meteors* come of a dry *exhalation*, which, being gotten enclosed within a moist cloud, striveth forcibly to get forth: now, by attrition and breaking together, it causeth the clap of thunder." Shakespeare has *meteor* repeatedly in the same way. So in *Romeo and Juliet*, iii. 5: "It is some *meteor* that the Sun *exhales*."

[146] Here the Poet had in his eye the following from Plutarch: "For Brutus, his friends and countrymen, both by divers procurements and sundry rumours of the city, and by many bills also, did openly call and procure him to do that he did. For, under the image of his ancestor Junius Brutus, that drave the kings out of Rome, they wrote, 'O, that it pleased the gods thou wert now alive, Brutus!' and again, 'That thou wert here among us now!' His tribunal or chair, where he gave audience during the time he was Prastor, was full of such bills: 'Brutus, thou art asleep, and art not Brutus indeed.'"

And the first motion,[147] all the interim is
Like a phantasma[148] or a hideous dream:
The Genius and the mortal instruments
Are then in council;[149] and the state of man,
Like to a little kingdom, suffers then
The nature of an insurrection.[150]

[*Re-enter* LUCIUS.]

LUCIUS. Sir, 'tis your brother Cassius at the door,
    Who doth desire to see you.
BRUTUS. Is he alone?
LUCIUS. No, sir, there are more with him.
BRUTUS. Do you know them?
LUCIUS. No, sir; their hats are pluck'd about their ears,
    And half their faces buried in their cloaks,
    That by no means I may discover them
    By any mark of favour.
BRUTUS. Let 'em enter.—[*Exit* LUCIUS.]
    They are the faction.—O conspiracy,
    Shamest thou to show thy dangerous brow by night,
    When evils are most free?[151] O, then by day
    Where wilt thou find a cavern dark enough
    To mask thy monstrous visage? Seek none, conspiracy;

---

[147] *Motion* for *impulse*, or the first budding of thought into purpose.

[148] A *phantasma* is a *phantom*; something imagined or fancied; a vision of things that are not, as in a nightmare.

[149] Commentators differ about *genius* here; some taking it for the *conscience*, others for the *anti-conscience*. Shakespeare uses *genius, spirit,* and *demon* as synonymous, and all three, apparently, both in a good sense and in a bad; as every man was supposed to have a good and a bad angel. So, in this play, we have "thy *evil spirit*"; in *The Tempest,* "our *worser genius*"; in *Troilus and Cressida,* "Some say *the genius* so cries Come! to him that instantly must die"; in *Antony and Cleopatra,* "Thy *demon,* that's thy *spirit* which keeps thee"; where, as often, *keeps* is *guards.* In these and some other cases, the words have some epithet or context that determines their meaning; but not so with *genius* in the text. But, in all such cases, the words, I think, mean the *directive* power of the mind. And so we often speak of a man's *better self,* or a man's *worser self,* according as one is in fact *directed* or *drawn* to good or to evil.—The sense of *mortal,* here, is also somewhat in question. The Poet sometimes uses it for *perishable,* or that which *dies;* but oftener for *deadly,* or that which *kills. Mortal instruments* may well be held to mean the same as when Macbeth says, "I'm settled, and bend up each *corporal agent* to this terrible feat."—As Brutus is speaking with reference to his own case, he probably intends *genius* in a good sense; for the spiritual or immortal part of himself. If so, then he would naturally mean, by *mortal,* his perishable part, or his *ministerial* faculties, which shrink from executing what the *directive* power is urging them to.

[150] That is, a *kind* of insurrection, or *something like* an insurrection.

[151] When *crimes* and *mischiefs,* or rather when evil and mischievous *men* are most free from the restraints of law, or of shame. So Hamlet speaks of night as the time "when Hell itself breathes out contagion to this world."

Hide it in smiles and affability:
For if thou path, thy native semblance on,[152]
Not Erebus itself were dim enough
To hide thee from prevention.[153]

[*Enter* CASSIUS, CASCA, DECIUS BRUTUS, CINNA,
METELLUS CIMBER, *and* TREBONIUS.]

CASSIUS. I think we are too bold upon your rest:
Good morrow, Brutus; do we trouble you?
BRUTUS. I have been up this hour, awake all night.
Know I these men that come along with you?
CASSIUS. Yes, every man of them, and no man here
But honours you; and every one doth wish
You had but that opinion of yourself
Which every noble Roman bears of you.
This is Trebonius.
BRUTUS. He is welcome hither.
CASSIUS. This, Decius[154] Brutus.
BRUTUS. He is welcome too.
CASSIUS. This, Casca; this, Cinna; and this, Metellus Cimber.
BRUTUS. They are all welcome.—
What watchful cares do interpose themselves
Betwixt your eyes and night?
CASSIUS. Shall I entreat a word?

[BRUTUS *and* CASSIUS *whisper.*]

DECIUS BRUTUS. Here lies the east: doth not the day break here?
CASCA. No.
CINNA. O, pardon, sir, it doth; and yon gray lines
That fret the clouds are messengers of day.
CASCA. You shall confess that you are both deceived.

[*He points his sword.*]

Here, as I point my sword, the sun arises,

---

[152] "Thy native semblance *being* on." Ablative absolute again.
[153] "To hide thee from *discovery*" which would lead to prevention.—Erebus was the darkest and gloomiest region of Hades. The meaning of the word is *darkness.*
[154] Shakespeare found the name thus in Plutarch. In fact, however, it was *Decimus,* not *Decius.* The man is said to have been cousin to the other Brutus of the play. He had been one of Cæsar's ablest, most favoured, and most trusted lieutenants, and had particularly distinguished himself in his naval service at Venetia and Massilia. After the murder of Cæsar, he was found to be written down in his will as second heir.

Which is a great way growing on the south,
Weighing the youthful season of the year.[155]
Some two months hence up higher toward the north
He first presents his fire; and the high east
Stands, as the Capitol, directly here.[156]

[*He points his sword.*]

[BRUTUS *and* CASSIUS *join the* CONSPIRATORS.]

BRUTUS. Give me your hands all over, one by one.

[*Shakes their hands.*]

CASSIUS. *And let us swear our resolution.*
BRUTUS. No, not an oath: if not the face of men,[157]
The sufferance of our souls, the time's abuse,—
If these be motives weak, break off betimes,
And every man hence to his idle bed;
So let high-sighted tyranny range on,
Till each man drop by lottery.[158] But if these,
As I am sure they do, bear fire enough
To kindle cowards and to steel with valour
The melting spirits of women, then, countrymen,
What[159] need we any spur but our own cause,
To prick us to redress? what other bond
Than secret Romans, that have spoke the word,
And will not palter?[160] and what other oath
Than honesty to honesty engaged,[161]
That this shall be, or we will fall for it?

---

[155] That is, *verging* or *inclining towards* the South, *in accordance with* the early time of the year. *Weighing* is considering.

[156] "The *high* East" is the *perfect* East. So the Poet has "*high* morning" for *morning full-blown.*—This little side-talk on an indifferent theme is finely conceived, and serves the double purpose of showing that they are not listening, and of preventing suspicion, if any were listening to them.

[157] Meaning, probably, the shame and self-reproach with which Romans must now *look each other in the face*, under the consciousness of having fallen away from the republican spirit of their forefathers.

[158] Brutus seems to have in mind the capriciousness of a high-looking and heaven-daring oriental tyranny, where men's lives hung upon the nod and whim of the tyrant, as on the hazards of a lottery.

[159] *What* for *why.* The Poet often has it so. And so in St. Mark, xiv. 63: "*What* need we any further witnesses?"

[160] To *palter* is to *equivocate*, to *shuffle*, as in making a promise with what is called "a mental reservation."

[161] *Engaged* is *pledged*, or *put in pawn.* A frequent usage.

Swear priests and cowards and men cautelous,[162]
Old feeble carrions,[163] and such suffering souls
That welcome wrongs; unto bad causes swear
Such creatures as men doubt; but do not stain
The even virtue[164] of our enterprise,
Nor th' insuppressive mettle of our spirits,
To think[165] that or our cause or our performance
Did need an oath; when every drop of blood
That every Roman bears, and nobly bears,
Is guilty of a several bastardy,
If he do break the smallest particle
Of any promise that hath pass'd from him.
CASSIUS. But what of Cicero? shall we sound him?
I think he will stand very strong with us.
CASCA. Let us not leave him out.
CINNA. No, by no means.
METELLUS CIMBER. O, let us have him, for his silver hairs
Will purchase us a good opinion,[166]
And buy men's voices to commend our deeds:
It shall be said, his judgment ruled our hands;
Our youths and wildness shall no whit appear,
But all be buried in his gravity.
BRUTUS. O, name him not: let us not break with him;[167]
For he will never follow any thing
That other men begin.
CASSIUS. Then leave him out.
CASCA. Indeed he is not fit.
DECIUS BRUTUS. Shall no man else be touch'd but only Cæsar?
CASSIUS. Decius, well urged: I think it is not meet,
Mark Antony, so well beloved of Cæsar,

---

[162] *Cautelous* is here used in the sense of *deceit* or fraud; though its original meaning is *wary, circumspect,* the same as *cautious.* The word is said to have caught a bad sense in passing through French hands. But, as the Clarendon edition notes, "the transition from caution to suspicion, and from suspicion to craft and deceit, is not very abrupt."

[163] *Carrions* for *carcasses,* or men as good as dead. Repeatedly so.

[164] Meaning the virtue that holds an equable and uniform tenour, always keeping the same high level.—*Insuppressive* for *insuppressible;* the active form with the passive sense.

[165] *By* thinking. The infinitive used gerundively again.

[166] *Opinion* for *reputation* or *estimation.* Often so. Observe the thread of association in *silver, purchase,* and *buy.*

[167] Old language for "let us not break *the matter to* him."—This bit of dialogue is very charming. Brutus knows full well that Cicero is not the man to play second fiddle to any of *them;* that if he have any thing to do with the enterprise it must be as the leader of it; and that is just what Brutus wants to be himself. Merivale thinks it a great honour to Cicero, that the conspirators did not venture to propose the matter to him.

Should outlive Cæsar: we shall find of him[168]
A shrewd contriver; and, you know, his means,
If he improve them, may well stretch so far
As to annoy us all: which to prevent,
Let Antony and Cæsar fall together.
BRUTUS. Our course will seem too bloody, Caius Cassius,
To cut the head off and then hack the limbs,
Like wrath in death and envy[169] afterwards;
For Antony is but a limb of Cæsar:
Let us be sacrificers, but not butchers, Caius.
We all stand up against the spirit of Cæsar;
And in the spirit of men there is no blood:
O, that we then could come by Cæsar's spirit,
And not dismember Cæsar! But, alas,
Cæsar must bleed for it! And, gentle friends,
Let's kill him boldly, but not wrathfully;
Let's carve him as a dish fit for the gods,
Not hew him as a carcass fit for hounds:
And let our hearts, as subtle masters do,
Stir up their servants to an act of rage,
And after seem to chide 'em.[170] This shall make
Our purpose necessary,[171] and not envious:
Which so appearing to the common eyes,
We shall be call'd purgers,[172] not murderers.
And for Mark Antony, think not of him;
For he can do no more than Cæsar's arm
When Cæsar's head is off.
CASSIUS. Yet I fear him;
For in the ingrafted love he bears to Cæsar—
BRUTUS. Alas, good Cassius, do not think of him:
If he love Cæsar, all that he can do
Is to himself, take thought and die for Cæsar:[173]
And that were much he should; for he is given

---

[168] We should say "find *in* him." So in *The Merchant*, iii. 5: "Even such a husband hast thou *of me* as she is for a wife."

[169] Here, as commonly in Shakespeare, *envy* is *malice* or *hatred.* And so, a little after, *envious* is *malicious.*—Here, again, *to cut* and *to hack* are gerundial infinitives.

[170] So the King proceeds with Hubert in *King John.* And so men often proceed when they wish to have a thing done, and to shirk the responsibility; setting it on by dark hints and allusions, and then, after it is done, affecting to blame or to scold the doers of it.

[171] That is, "*will* mark our purpose *as* necessary," or the offspring of necessity. The indiscriminate use of *shall* and *will* is frequent.

[172] Meaning *healers*, who cleanse the land from the disease of tyranny.

[173] "Think and die," or "take thought and die," is an old phrase for *grieve one's self to death*: and it would be much indeed, a very wonderful thing, if Antony should fall into any killing sorrow, such a light-hearted, jolly companion as he is. So the Poet uses *think* and *thought* repeatedly.

To sports, to wildness and much company.

TREBONIUS. There is no fear in him;[174] let him not die;

For he will live, and laugh at this hereafter. [*Clock strikes.*]

BRUTUS. Peace! count the clock.

CASSIUS. The clock hath stricken three.

TREBONIUS. 'Tis time to part.

CASSIUS. But it is doubtful yet,

Whether Cæsar will come forth to-day, or no;

For he is superstitious grown of late,

Quite from the main[175] opinion he held once

Of fantasy, of dreams and ceremonies.[176]

It may be, these apparent[177] prodigies,

The unaccustom'd terror of this night,

And the persuasion of his augurers,

May hold him from the Capitol to-day.

DECIUS BRUTUS. Never fear that: if he be so resolved,

I can o'ersway him; for he loves to hear

That unicorns may be betray'd with trees,

And bears with glasses, elephants with holes,

Lions with toils,[178] and men with flatterers;

But when I tell him he hates flatterers,

He says he does, being then most flattered.

Let me work;

For I can give his humour the true bent,

And I will bring him to the Capitol.

CASSIUS. Nay, we will all of us be there to fetch him.

BRUTUS. By the eighth hour: is that the uttermost?

CINNA. Be that the uttermost, and fail not then.

METELLUS CIMBER. Caius Ligarius doth bear Cæsar hard,

---

[174] No fear *on account of* him, or *because of* him, is the meaning. So *in* is used in several other places.

[175] *Great, strong, mighty* are among the old senses of *main*. And *from*, in Shakespeare, often has the force of *contrary to*. So in Hamlet's saying, "is *from* the purpose of playing."

[176] Cæsar was, in his philosophy, an Epicurean, as most of the educated Romans then also were. Hence he was, in opinion, strongly sceptical about dreams and ceremonial auguries. Nevertheless, as is apt to be the case with sceptics and freethinkers, his conduct, especially in his later years, was marked with many gross instances of superstitious practice.

[177] *Apparent*, here, is *evident* or *manifest*. A frequent usage.

[178] The way to catch that fabulous old beast, the unicorn, is, to stand before a tree, and, when he runs at you, to slip aside, and let him stick his horn into the tree: then you have him. See *The Faerie Queene*, ii. 5, 10.—Bears are said to have been caught by putting looking-glasses in their way; they being so taken with the images of themselves, that the hunters could easily master them.—Elephants were beguiled into pitfalls, lightly covered over with hurdles and turf; a bait being placed thereon, to tempt them.—*Toil* is *trap* or *snare*. So in *Antony and Cleopatra*, v. 2: "As she would catch another Antony in her strong *toil* of grace."

Who rated him for speaking well of Pompey:
I wonder none of you have thought of him.
BRUTUS. Now, good Metellus, go along by him:[179]
   He loves me well, and I have given him reason;[180]
   Send him but hither, and I'll fashion him.
CASSIUS. The morning comes upon's: we'll leave you, Brutus.
   And, friends, disperse yourselves; but all remember
   What you have said, and show yourselves true Romans.
BRUTUS. Good gentlemen, look fresh and merrily;
   Let not our looks put on our purposes,[181]
   But bear it as our Roman actors do,
   With untired spirits and formal constancy:
   And so good morrow to you every one.—

   [*Exeunt all but* BRUTUS.]

   Boy! Lucius! Fast asleep? It is no matter;
   Enjoy the honey-heavy dew of slumber:[182]
   Thou hast no figures nor no fantasies,
   Which busy care draws in the brains of men;
   Therefore thou sleep'st so sound.

   [*Enter* PORTIA.]

PORTIA. Brutus, my lord!
BRUTUS. Portia, what mean you? wherefore rise you now?
   It is not for your health thus to commit
   Your weak condition to the raw cold morning.
PORTIA. Nor for yours neither. You've ungently, Brutus,
   Stole from my bed: and yesternight, at supper,
   You suddenly arose, and walk'd about,
   Musing and sighing, with your arms across,
   And when I ask'd you what the matter was,
   You stared upon me with ungentle looks;
   I urged you further; then you scratch'd your head,
   And too impatiently stamp'd with your foot;
   Yet I insisted, yet you answer'd not,

---

[179] That is, by his house: "make that your way home."

[180] The meaning probably is, "given him reason to love me."

[181] "Let not our looks betray our purposes by wearing, or being attired with, any indication of them."

[182] The compound epithet *honey-heavy* is very expressive and apt. The "dew of slumber" is called *heavy* because it makes the subject feel heavy, and *honey-heavy* because the heaviness it induces is sweet.—Brutus is naturally led to contrast the free and easy state of the boy's mind with that of his own, which the excitement of his present undertaking is drawing full of visions and images of trouble.

But, with an angry wafture of your hand,
Gave sign for me to leave you: so I did;
Fearing to strengthen that impatience
Which seem'd too much enkindled, and withal
Hoping it was but an effect of humour,
Which sometime hath his hour with every man.
It will not let you eat, nor talk, nor sleep,
And could it work so much upon your shape
As it hath much prevail'd on your condition,[183]
I should not know you, Brutus. Dear my lord,
Make me acquainted with your cause of grief.
BRUTUS. I am not well in health, and that is all.
PORTIA. Brutus is wise, and, were he not in health,
He would embrace the means to come by it.
BRUTUS. Why, so I do. Good Portia, go to bed.
PORTIA. Is Brutus sick? and is it physical[184]
To walk unbraced and suck up the humours
Of the dank morning? What, is Brutus sick,
And will he steal out of his wholesome bed,
To dare the vile contagion of the night
And tempt the rheumy[185] and unpurged air
To add unto his sickness? No, my Brutus;
You have some sick offence within your mind,
Which, by the right and virtue of my place,
I ought to know of: [*Kneeling.*] and, upon my knees,
I charm you, by my once-commended beauty,
By all your vows of love and that great vow
Which did incorporate and make us one,
That you unfold to me, yourself, your half,
Why you are heavy, and what men to-night
Have had to resort to you: for here have been
Some six or seven, who did hide their faces
Even from darkness.
BRUTUS. Kneel not, gentle Portia.
PORTIA. I should not need, if you were gentle Brutus.
Within the bond of marriage, tell me, Brutus,
Is it excepted I should know no secrets

---

[183] *Condition* was much used for *temper* or *disposition*. The term *ill-conditioned* is still in use for a cross-grained, irascible, or quarrelsome disposition, or an ugly temper.
[184] The Poet has *physical* again for *wholesome* or *medicinal*, in *Coriolanus*, i. 5: "The blood I drop is rather *physical* than dangerous to me."
[185] *Rheum* was specially used of the fluids that issue from the eyes or mouth. So in *Hamlet* we have "bisson *rheum*" for blinding *tears*. *Rheumy* here means that state of the air which causes the unhealthy issue of such fluids, or perhaps which makes people *rheumatic*. So, in *A Midsummer Night's Dream*, ii. 1, Titania speaks of the Moon as "washing all the air, that rheumatic diseases do abound."

That appertain to you? Am I yourself
But, as it were, in sort or limitation,
To keep with you at meals, comfort your bed,
And talk to you sometimes? Dwell I but in the suburbs
Of your good pleasure?[186] If it be no more,
Portia is Brutus' harlot, not his wife.
BRUTUS. You are my true and honourable wife,
    As dear to me as are the ruddy drops
    That visit my sad heart.[187]
PORTIA. If this were true, then should I know this secret.
    I grant I am a woman; but withal
    A woman that Lord Brutus took to wife:
    I grant I am a woman; but withal
    A woman well-reputed, Cato's daughter.
    Think you I am no stronger than my sex,
    Being so father'd and so husbanded?
    Tell me your counsels, I will not disclose 'em:
    I have made strong proof of my constancy,
    Giving myself a voluntary wound
    Here, in the thigh: can I bear that with patience.
    And not my husband's secrets?
BRUTUS. O ye gods,
    Render me worthy of this noble wife!—[*Knocking within.*]
    Hark, hark! one knocks: Portia, go in awhile;
    And by and by thy bosom shall partake
    The secrets of my heart.
    All my engagements I will construe to thee,
    All the charactery of my sad brows:[188]
    Leave me with haste. [*Exit* PORTIA.]—Lucius, who's that
    knocks?

[*Re-enter* LUCIUS *with* LIGARIUS.]

LUCIUS. He is a sick man that would speak with you.
BRUTUS. Caius Ligarius, that Metellus spake of.
    Boy, stand aside. Caius Ligarius! how?

---

[186] In the outskirts or borders, and not at the centre or near the heart. The image is exceeding apposite and expressive.

[187] This embodies what was then known touching the circulation of the blood. William Harvey was born in 1578, fourteen years after Shakespeare, and his discovery was not published till 1628, twelve years after the Poet's death. The general fact of the circulation of the blood was known in ancient times; and Harvey's discovery lay in ascertaining the *modus operandi* of it, and in reducing it to matter of strict science.

[188] *Charactery* is defined "writing by characters or strange marks." Brutus therefore means that he will divulge to her the secret cause of the sadness marked on his countenance.

LIGARIUS. Vouchsafe good morrow from a feeble tongue.
BRUTUS. O, what a time have you chose out, brave Caius,
To wear a kerchief!¹⁸⁹ Would you were not sick!
LIGARIUS. I am not sick, if Brutus have in hand
Any exploit worthy the name of honour.
BRUTUS. Such an exploit have I in hand, Ligarius,
Had you a healthful ear to hear of it.
LIGARIUS. By all the gods that Romans bow before,
I here discard my sickness!

[*Pulls off his kerchief.*]

Soul of Rome!
Brave son, derived from honourable loins!
Thou, like an exorcist,¹⁹⁰ hast conjured up
My mortified spirit.¹⁹¹ Now bid me run,
And I will strive with things impossible;
Yea, get the better of them. What's to do?
BRUTUS. A piece of work that will make sick men whole.
LIGARIUS. But are not some whole that we must make sick?
BRUTUS. That must we also. What it is, my Caius,
I shall unfold to thee, as we are going
To whom it must be done.
LIGARIUS. Set on your foot,
And with a heart new-fired I follow you,
To do I know not what: but it sufficeth
That Brutus leads me on.
BRUTUS. Follow me, then. [*Exeunt.*]

SCENE II.

The Same. A Hall in CÆSAR's *Palace.*

[*Thunder and lightning. Enter* CÆSAR, *in his night-gown.*]

CÆSAR. Nor heaven nor earth have been at peace to-night:
Thrice hath Calpurnia in her sleep cried out,

---

¹⁸⁹ It was a common practice in England for those who were sick to wear a kerchief on their heads. So in Fuller's *Worthies of Cheshire*: "If any there be sick, they make him a posset and *tye a kerchief on his head*; and if that will not mend him, then God be merciful to him."

¹⁹⁰ In Shakespeare's time, *exorcist* and *conjurer* were used indifferently. The former has since come to mean only one who drives away spirits; the latter, one who calls them up.

¹⁹¹ That is, "my spirit which was dead in me." Such is the literal meaning of *mortified*; and so the Poet has it repeatedly.

Help, ho! *they murder Cæsar*!—Who's within?

[*Enter a* SERVANT.]

SERVANT. My lord?
CÆSAR. Go bid the priests do present sacrifice
    And bring me their opinions of success.[192]
SERVANT. I will, my lord. [*Exit.*]

[*Enter* CALPURNIA.]

CALPURNIA. What mean you, Cæsar? think you to walk forth?
    You shall not stir out of your house to-day.
CÆSAR. Cæsar shall forth: the things that threaten me
    Ne'er look'd but on my back; when they shall see
    The face of Cæsar, they are vanished.
CALPURNIA. Cæsar, I never stood on ceremonies,[193]
    Yet now they fright me. There is one within,
    Besides the things that we have heard and seen,
    Recounts most horrid sights seen by the watch.
    A lioness hath whelped in the streets;
    And graves have yawn'd, and yielded up their dead;
    Fierce fiery warriors fought upon the clouds,
    In ranks and squadrons and right form of war,
    Which drizzled blood upon the Capitol;
    The noise of battle hurtled[194] in the air,
    Horses did neigh, and dying men did groan,
    And ghosts did shriek and squeal about the streets.
    O Cæsar! these things are beyond all use,
    And I do fear them.
CÆSAR. What can be avoided
    Whose end is purposed by the mighty gods?
    Yet Cæsar shall go forth; for these predictions
    Are to the world in general as to Cæsar.
CALPURNIA. When beggars die, there are no comets seen;
    The heavens themselves blaze forth the death of princes.
CÆSAR. Cowards die many times before their deaths;
    The valiant never taste of death but once.[195]

---

[192] Their opinions of what is to *follow*. The Poet often uses *success* in this sense.

[193] *Ceremonies* is here put for the ceremonial or sacerdotal interpretation of prodigies and omens.

[194] To *hurtle* is to clash, or move with violence and noise.

[195] Plutarch relates that, a short time before Cæsar fell, some of his friends urged him to have a guard about him, and he replied that it was better to die at once than live in the continual fear of death. He is also said to have given as his reason for refusing a

Of all the wonders that I yet have heard.
It seems to me most strange that men should fear;
Seeing that death, a necessary end,
Will come when it will come.—

[*Re-enter* SERVANT.]

What say the augurers?
SERVANT. They would not have you to stir forth to-day.
Plucking the entrails of an offering forth,
They could not find a heart within the beast.
CÆSAR. The gods do this in shame of cowardice:
Cæsar should be a beast without a heart,
If he should stay at home to-day for fear.
No, Cæsar shall not: danger knows full well
That Cæsar is more dangerous than he:
We are two lions litter'd in one day,
And I the elder and more terrible:
And Cæsar shall go forth.
CALPURNIA. Alas, my lord,
Your wisdom is consumed in confidence.
Do not go forth to-day: call it my fear
That keeps you in the house, and not your own.
We'll send Mark Antony to the senate-house:
And he shall say you are not well to-day:
Let me, upon my knee, prevail in this.
CÆSAR. Mark Antony shall say I am not well,
And, for thy humour, I will stay at home.

[*Enter* DECIUS BRUTUS.]

Here's Decius Brutus, he shall tell them so.
DECIUS BRUTUS. Cæsar, all hail! good morrow, worthy Cæsar:
I come to fetch you to the senate-house.
CÆSAR. And you are come in very happy time,
To bear my greeting to the senators
And tell them that I will not come to-day:
Cannot, is false, and that I dare not, falser:
I will not come to-day: tell them so, Decius.
CALPURNIA. Say he is sick.
CÆSAR. Shall Cæsar send a lie?

---

guard, that he thought Rome had more need of him than he of Rome; which was indeed
true. And it is further stated that, on the eve of the fatal day, Cæsar being at the house of
Lepidus with some friends, and the question being raised, "What kind of death is best?"
he cut short the discussion by saying, "That which is least expected."

Have I in conquest stretch'd mine arm so far,
To be afraid to tell graybeards the truth?—
Decius, go tell them Cæsar will not come.
DECIUS BRUTUS. Most mighty Cæsar, let me know some cause,
Lest I be laugh'd at when I tell them so.
CÆSAR. The cause is in my will: I will not come;
That is enough to satisfy the senate.
But for your private satisfaction,
Because I love you, I will let you know:
Calpurnia here, my wife, stays me at home:
She dreamt to-night she saw my statua,[196]
Which, like a fountain with an hundred spouts,
Did run pure blood: and many lusty Romans
Came smiling, and did bathe their hands in it:
And these does she apply for warnings, and portents,
And evils imminent; and on her knee
Hath begg'd that I will stay at home to-day.
DECIUS BRUTUS. This dream is all amiss interpreted;
It was a vision fair and fortunate:
Your statue spouting blood in many pipes,
In which so many smiling Romans bathed,
Signifies that from you great Rome shall suck
Reviving blood, and that great men shall press
For tinctures, stains, relics and cognizance.[197]
This by Calpurnia's dream is signified.
CÆSAR. And this way have you well expounded it.
DECIUS BRUTUS. I have, when you have heard what I can say:
And know it now: the senate have concluded
To give this day a crown to mighty Cæsar.[198]
If you shall send them word you will not come,
Their minds may change. Besides, it were a mock
Apt to be render'd,[199] for some one to say

---

[196] In Shakespeare's time *statue* was pronounced indifferently as a word of two syllables or three. Bacon uses it repeatedly as a trisyllable, and spells it *statua*, as in his *Advancement of Learning*: "It is not possible to have the true pictures or *statuas* of Cyrus, Alexander, Cæsar, no, nor of the kings or great personages of much later years."

[197] *Cognizance* is here used in a heraldic sense, as meaning any badge or token to show whose friends or servants the owners or wearers were. In ancient times, when martyrs or other distinguished men were executed, their friends often *pressed* to stain handkerchiefs with their blood, or to get some other relic, which they might keep, either as precious memorials of them, or as having a kind of sacramental virtue.

[198] The Roman people were specially yearning to avenge the slaughter of Marcus Crassus and his army by the Parthians; and Cæsar was at this time preparing an expedition against them. But a Sibylline oracle was alleged, that Parthia could only be conquered by a king; and it was proposed to invest Cæsar with the royal title and authority over the foreign subjects of the State.

[199] It were apt, or likely, to be *construed* or *represented* as a piece of mockery. So

Break up the senate till another time,
When Cæsar's wife shall meet with better dreams.
If Cæsar hide himself, shall they not whisper
Lo, Cæsar is afraid?
Pardon me, Cæsar; for my dear dear love
To our proceeding bids me tell you this;
And reason to my love is liable.[200]
CÆSAR. How foolish do your fears seem now, Calpurnia!
I am ashamed I did yield to them.
Give me my robe, for I will go.

[*Enter* PUBLIUS, BRUTUS, LIGARIUS, METELLUS, CASCA,
TREBONIUS, *and* CINNA.]

And look where Publius[201] is come to fetch me.
PUBLIUS. Good morrow, Cæsar.
CÆSAR. Welcome, Publius.
What, Brutus, are you stirr'd so early too?
Good morrow, Casca. Caius Ligarius,
Cæsar was ne'er so much your enemy
As that same ague which hath made you lean.[202]—
What is't o'clock?
BRUTUS. Cæsar, 'tis strucken eight.
CÆSAR. I thank you for your pains and courtesy.

[*Enter* ANTONY.]

See! Antony, that revels long o' nights,
Is notwithstanding up.—Good morrow, Antony.
ANTONY. So to most noble Cæsar.
CÆSAR. Bid them prepare within:
I am to blame to be thus waited for.—
Now, Cinna;—now, Metellus;—what, Trebonius!
I have an hour's talk in store for you;
Remember that you call on me to-day:
Be near me, that I may remember you.
TREBONIUS. Cæsar, I will;—[*Aside.*] and so near will I be,

---

the Poet repeatedly uses the verb to *render.*
[200] The thought here is, that love stands as principal, reason as second or subordinate. "The deference which reason holds due from me to you is in this instance *subject* and *amenable* to the calls of personal affection."
[201] This was Publius Silicius; not one of the conspirators.
[202] Here, for the first time, we have Cæsar speaking fairly in character; for he was probably the most finished gentleman of his time, one of the sweetest of men, and as full of kindness as of wisdom and courage. Merivale aptly styles him "Cæsar the politic and the merciful."

That your best friends shall wish I had been further.
CÆSAR. Good friends, go in, and taste some wine with me;
    And we, like friends, will straightway go together.
BRUTUS. [*Aside.*] That every like is not the same, O Cæsar,
    The heart of Brutus yearns to think upon![203] [*Exeunt.*]

SCENE III.

The Same. A Street near the Capitol.

[*Enter* ARTEMIDORUS, *reading a paper.*]

ARTEMIDORUS. *Cæsar, beware of Brutus; take heed of Cassius;
come not near Casca; have an eye to Cinna, trust not Trebonius:
mark well Metellus Cimber: Decius Brutus loves thee not: thou
hast wronged Caius Ligarius. There is but one mind in all these
men, and it is bent against Cæsar. If thou beest not immortal, look
about you: security gives way to conspiracy.[204] The mighty gods
defend thee!*

                    Thy lover,   ARTEMIDORUS.

    Here will I stand till Cæsar pass along,
    And as a suitor will I give him this.
    My heart laments that virtue cannot live
    Out of the teeth of emulation.[205]—
    If thou read this, O Cæsar, thou mayst live;
    If not, the Fates with traitors do contrive. [*Exit.*]

SCENE IV.

*The Same. Another Part of the same Street,
before the house of* BRUTUS.

[*Enter* PORTIA *and* LUCIUS.]

PORTIA. I prithee, boy, run to the senate-house;
    Stay not to answer me, but get thee gone:

---

[203] The winning and *honest* suavity of Cæsar here starts a pang of remorse in
Brutus. Drinking wine together was regarded as a sacred pledge of truth and honour.
Brutus knows that Cæsar is doing it in good faith; and it hurts him to think that the others
seem to be doing the *like*, and yet are doing a very different thing. To *yearn* is to *grieve*,
to *be pained.* Repeatedly used so by the Poet.
  [204] *Negligence* or *over-confidence makes* or *opens* a way for conspiracy. The use of
security and *secure* in this sense is very frequent.
  [205] *Emulation* is *factious* and *envious rivalry.* So in *Troilus and Cressida,* i. 3: "An
envious fever of pale and bloodless *emulation.*"

Why dost thou stay?

LUCIUS. To know my errand, madam.

PORTIA. I would have had thee there, and here again,
  Ere I can tell thee what thou shouldst do there.
  O constancy, be strong upon my side,
  Set a huge mountain 'tween my heart and tongue!
  I have a man's mind, but a woman's might.
  How hard it is for women to keep counsel!
  Art thou here yet?

LUCIUS. Madam, what should I do?
  Run to the Capitol, and nothing else?
  And so return to you, and nothing else?

PORTIA. Yes, bring me word, boy, if thy lord look well,
  For he went sickly forth: and take good note
  What Cæsar doth, what suitors press to him.
  Hark, boy! what noise is that?

LUCIUS. I hear none, madam.

PORTIA. Prithee, listen well;
  I heard a bustling rumour,[206] like a fray,
  And the wind brings it from the Capitol.

LUCIUS. Sooth,[207] madam, I hear nothing.

[*Enter the* SOOTHSAYER.]

PORTIA. Come hither, fellow: which way hast thou been?

SOOTHSAYER. At mine own house, good lady.

PORTIA. What is't o'clock?

SOOTHSAYER. About the ninth hour, lady.

PORTIA. Is Cæsar yet gone to the Capitol?

SOOTHSAYER. Madam, not yet: I go to take my stand,
  To see him pass on to the Capitol.

PORTIA. Thou hast some suit to Cæsar, hast thou not?

SOOTHSAYER. That I have, lady: if it will please Cæsar
  To be so good to Cæsar as to hear me,
  I shall beseech him to befriend himself.

PORTIA. Why, know'st thou any harm's intended towards him?

SOOTHSAYER. None that I know will be, much that I fear may chance.
  Good morrow to you.—Here the street is narrow:
  The throng that follows Cæsar at the heels,

---

[206] A *loud noise* or *murmur*, as of stir and tumult, is one of the old meanings of *rumour.*—Since the interview of Brutus and Portia, he has unbosomed all his secrets to her; and now she is in such a fever of anxiety, that she mistakes her fancies for facts.

[207] *Sooth* for *in sooth*; that is, *in truth*, or *truly.* A *soothsayer* is, properly, a *truth-speaker.* So the Poet often uses *sooth.*

Of senators, of prætors, common suitors,
Will crowd a feeble man almost to death:
I'll get me to a place more void, and there
Speak to great Cæsar as he comes along. [*Exit.*]
PORTIA. I must go in.—[*Aside.*] Ay me, how weak a thing
The heart of woman is!—O Brutus,
The heavens speed thee in thine enterprise!—
Sure, the boy heard me:—Brutus hath a suit
That Cæsar will not grant.[208]—O, I grow faint.—
Run, Lucius, and commend me to my lord;
Say I am merry: come to me again,
And bring me word what he doth say to thee.

[*Exeunt severally.*]

ACT III.

SCENE I.

Rome. Before the Capitol; the Senate sitting.

[*A crowd of people in the street leading to the Capitol; among them* ARTEMIDORUS *and the* SOOTHSAYER. *Flourish. Enter* CÆSAR, BRUTUS, CASSIUS, CASCA, DECIUS BRUTUS, METELLUS CIMBER, TREBONIUS, CINNA, ANTONY, LEPIDUS, POPILLIUS, PUBLIUS, *and others.*]

CÆSAR. The Ides of March are come.
SOOTHSAYER. Ay, Cæsar; but not gone.[209]
ARTEMIDORUS. Hail, Cæsar! Read this schedule.
DECIUS BRUTUS. Trebonius doth desire you to o'erread,
At your best leisure, this his humble suit.
ARTEMIDORUS. O Cæsar, read mine first; for mine's a suit
That touches Cæsar nearer: read it, great Cæsar.
CÆSAR. What touches us ourself shall be last served.
ARTEMIDORUS. Delay not, Cæsar; read it instantly.[210]

---

[208] These words Portia speaks aloud to Lucius, as a blind to cover the true cause of her uncontrollable flutter of spirits.

[209] There was a certain soothsayer, that had given Cæsar warning long time afore, to take heed of the day of the Ides of March, which is the 15th of the month; for on that day he should be in great danger. That day being come, Cæsar, going into the Senate-house, and speaking merrily unto the soothsayer, told him "the Ides of March be come."—"So they be," softly answered the soothsayer, "but yet are they not past."—PLUTARCH.

[210] One Artemidorus also, born in the isle of Cnidos, a doctor of rhetoric in the Greek tongue, who by means of his profession was very familiar with certain of Brutus's confederates, and therefore knew the most part of all their practices against Cæsar, came

CÆSAR. What, is the fellow mad?
PUBLIUS. Sirrah, give place.
CASSIUS. What, urge you your petitions in the street?
    Come to the Capitol.[211]

[CÆSAR *enters Capitol, the rest following. All the* SENATORS *rise.*]

POPILLIUS. I wish your enterprise to-day may thrive.
CASSIUS. What enterprise, Popillius?
POPILLIUS. Fare you well.

[*Advances to* CÆSAR.]

BRUTUS. What said Popillius Lena?
CASSIUS. He wish'd to-day our enterprise might thrive.
    I fear our purpose is discovered.
BRUTUS. Look, how he makes to Cæsar; mark him.
CASSIUS. Casca, be sudden, for we fear prevention.—
    Brutus, what shall be done? If this be known,
    Cassius or Cæsar never shall turn back,[212]
    For I will slay myself.
BRUTUS. Cassius, be constant:
    Popillius Lena speaks not of our purposes;
    For, look, he smiles, and Cæsar doth not change.[213]

---

and brought him a little bill, written with his own hand, of all that he meant to tell him. He, marking how Cæsar received all the supplications that were offered him, and that he gave them straight to his men that were about him, pressed nearer to him, and said: "Cæsar, read this memorial to yourself, and that quickly, for they be matters of great weight, and touch you nearly."—PLUTARCH.

[211] The murder of Cæsar did not, in fact, take place in the Capitol, but in a hall or *Curia* adjoining Pompey's theatre, where a statute of Pompey had been erected. The Senate had various places of meeting; generally in the Capitol, occasionally in some one of the Temples, at other times in one of the Curiae, of which there were several in and about the city.

[212] The meaning evidently is, "cither Cassius or Cæsar shall never return alive; for, if I do not kill him, I will slay myself."

[213] A senator called Popilius Lena, after he had saluted Brutus and Cassius more friendly than he was wont to do, he rounded softly in their ears, and told them, "I pray the gods you may go through with that you have taken in hand; but, withal, dispatch, I read you, for your enterprise is bewrayed." When he had said, he presently departed from them, and left them both afraid that their conspiracy would out.—When Cæsar came out of the litter, Popilius Lena went unto him, and kept him a long time with talk. Cæsar gave good ear unto him; wherefore the conspirators, not hearing what he said, but conjecturing that his talk was none other but the very discovery of their conspiracy, they were afraid every man of them; and, one looking in another's face, it was easy to see that they all were of a mind that it was no tarrying for them till they were apprehended, but rather that they should kill themselves with their own hands.—PLUTARCH.

CASSIUS. Trebonius knows his time; for, look you, Brutus.
 He draws Mark Antony out of the way.

 [*Exeunt* ANTONY *and* TREBONIUS. CÆSAR *and the*
  SENATORS *take their seats.*]

DECIUS BRUTUS. Where is Metellus Cimber? Let him go,
 And presently prefer his suit to Cæsar.
BRUTUS. He is address'd:[214] press near and second him.
CINNA. Casca, you are the first that rears your hand.
CÆSAR. Are we all ready? What is now amiss
 That Cæsar and his senate must redress?
METELLUS CIMBER. Most high, most mighty, and most puissant
  Cæsar,
 Metellus Cimber throws before thy seat
 An humble heart,—[*Kneeling.*]
CÆSAR. I must prevent thee, Cimber.
 These couchings[215] and these lowly courtesies
 Might fire the blood of ordinary men,
 And turn pre-ordinance and first decree
 Into the law of children.[216] Be not fond,
 To think[217] that Cæsar bears such rebel blood
 That will be thaw'd from the true quality
 With that which melteth fools; I mean, sweet words,
 Low-crooked court'sies and base spaniel-fawning.
 Thy brother by decree is banished:
 If thou dost bend and pray and fawn for him,
 I spurn thee like a cur out of my way.
METELLUS CIMBER. Cæsar, thou dost wrong.
CÆSAR. Cæsar did not wrong but with just cause,[218]
 Nor without cause will he be satisfied.

---

[214] *Address'd* is *ready* ox *prepared.* Often so.

[215] Among the proper senses of to *couch*, Richardson gives "to lower, to stoop, to bend down"; and he says that "to *couch* and to *lower* have similar applications, and probably the same origin."

[216] "Pre-ordinance and first decree" is, I take it, the ruling or enactment of the highest authority in the State. "The play of children" here referred to is, as soon as they have done a thing, to turn round and undo it, or to build a house of blocks or cobs for the mere fun of knocking it over.

[217] "Be not *so* fond *as* to think," is the language in full. The Poet often omits the adverbs in such cases. *Fond*, here, is *foolish*; which was its ordinary sense in Shakespeare's time.

[218] Metellus and Cæsar here use wrong in different senses. But to *hurt*, to *offend*, to *cause pain* were among its legitimate meanings in Shakespeare's time. So he has it afterwards in this play: "It shall advantage more than do us *wrong.*" And so in several other places; as in *Othello*, ii. 3: "I persuade myself, to speak the truth shall nothing *wrong* him." To *wring* and to *wrest* are from the same root as *wrong.*

METELLUS CIMBER. Is there no voice more worthy than my own
    To sound more sweetly in great Cæsar's ear
    For the repealing[219] of my banish'd brother?
BRUTUS. I kiss thy hand, but not in flattery, Cæsar;
    Desiring thee that Publius Cimber may
    Have an immediate freedom of repeal.
CÆSAR. What, Brutus!
CASSIUS. Pardon, Cæsar; Cæsar, pardon:
    As low as to thy foot doth Cassius fall,
    To beg enfranchisement for Publius Cimber.
CASSIUS. I could be well moved, if I were as you:
    If I could pray to move, prayers would move me:[220]
    But I am constant as the northern star,
    Of whose true-fix'd and resting quality
    There is no fellow in the firmament.
    The skies are painted with unnumber'd sparks,
    They are all fire and every one doth shine,
    But there's but one in all doth hold his place:
    So in the world; 'tis furnish'd well with men,
    And men are flesh and blood, and apprehensive;[221]
    Yet in the number I do know but one
    That unassailable holds on his rank,
    Unshaked of motion:[222] and that I am he,
    Let me a little show it, even in this;
    That I was constant Cimber should be banish'd,
    And constant do remain to keep him so.[223]
CINNA. O Cæsar,—
CÆSAR. Hence! Wilt thou lift up Olympus?
DECIUS BRUTUS. Great Cæsar,—
CÆSAR. Doth not Brutus bootless kneel?
CASCA. Speak, hands for me!

---

[219] To *repeal* from banishment is, in old English, to *recall* by repealing the sentence.

[220] "If I could seek to move others by prayers, then I were capable of being myself moved by the prayers of others."

[221] *Apprehensive* is *intelligent, capable of apprehending.*

[222] "Unshaked of motion" is simply *unmoved,* or *not subject to motion.* Undisturbed *by* the motion of others. As all readers of the Bible know, *of* was continually used, with passive verbs, to denote the agent.

[223] All through this scene, Cæsar is made to speak quite out of character, and in a strain of hateful arrogance, in order, apparently, to soften the enormity of his murder, and to grind the daggers of the assassins to a sharper point. Perhaps, also, it is a part of the irony which so marks this play, to put the haughtiest words in Cæsar's mouth just before his fall.

[CASCA *stabs* CÆSAR *in the neck.* CÆSAR *catches hold of his
    arm. He is then stabbed by several other Conspirators, and
    last by* MARCUS BRUTUS]

CÆSAR. Et tu, Brute?[224]—Then fall, Cæsar![225]

[*Dies. The* SENATORS *and* PEOPLE *retire in confusion.*]

CINNA. Liberty! Freedom! Tyranny is dead!
    Run hence, proclaim, cry it about the streets.
CASSIUS. Some to the common pulpits, and cry out
    Liberty, freedom, and enfranchisement![226]
BRUTUS. People and senators, be not affrighted;
    Fly not; stand stiff: ambition's debt is paid.
CASCA. Go to the pulpit, Brutus.
DECIUS BRUTUS. And Cassius too.
BRUTUS. Where's Publius?
CINNA. Here, quite confounded with this mutiny.
METELLUS CIMBER. Stand fast together, lest some friend of Cæsar's
    Should chance—
BRUTUS. Talk not of standing. Publius, good cheer;
    There is no harm intended to your person,
    Nor to no Roman else: so tell them, Publius.
CASSIUS. And leave us, Publius; lest that the people,
    Rushing on us, should do your age some mischief.
BRUTUS. Do so;—and let no man abide[227] this deed,

---

[224] There is no classical authority for putting these words into the mouth of Cæsar;
and the English equivalent, *Thou too, Brutus,* sounds so much better, that it seems a pity
the Poet did not write so. Cæsar had been as a father to Brutus, who was fifteen years his
junior; and the Greek, *Kai su teknon,* "You too, my son," which Dion and Suetonius put
into his mouth, though probably unauthentic, is good enough to be true.

[225] Then Cimber with both his hands plucked Cæsar's gown over his shoulders, and
Casca, that stood behind him, drew his dagger first and struck Cæsar upon the shoulder,
but gave him no great wound. Cæsar, feeling himself hurt, took him straight by the hand
he held his dagger in, and cried out in Latin: "O traitor Casca, what doest thou?" Casca
on the other side cried in Greek, and called his brother to help him. So divers running on
a heap together to fly upon Cæsar, he, looking about him to have fled, saw Brutus with a
sword drawn in his hand ready to strike at him: then he let Casca's hand go, and, casting
his gown over his face, suffered every man to strike at him that would. Then the
conspirators thronging one upon another, because every man was desirous to have a cut
at him, so many swords and daggers lighting upon one body, one of them hurt another,
and among them Brutus caught a blow on his hand, because he would make one in
murdering of him, and all the rest also were every man of them bloodied.—PLUTARCH.

[226] This is somewhat in the style of Caliban, when he gets glorious with "celestial
liquor," *The Tempest,* ii. 2: "Freedom, hey-day! hey-day, freedom! freedom, hey-day,
freedom!"

[227] To *abide* a thing is to be responsible for it, to bear the consequences.

But we the doers.

[*Re-enter* TREBONIUS.]

CASSIUS. Where is Antony?
TREBONIUS. Fled to his house amazed:
  Men, wives and children stare, cry out and run
  As it were doomsday.
BRUTUS. Fates, we will know your pleasures:
  That we shall die, we know; 'tis but the time
  And drawing days out, that men stand upon.[228]
CASSIUS. Why, he that cuts off twenty years of life
  Cuts off so many years of fearing death.
BRUTUS. Grant that, and then is death a benefit:
  So are we Cæsar's friends, that have abridged
  His time of fearing death. Stoop, Romans, stoop,
  And let us bathe our hands in Cæsar's blood
  Up to the elbows, and besmear our swords:
  Then walk we forth, even to the market-place,
  And, waving our red weapons o'er our heads,
  Let's all cry *Peace, freedom and liberty!*
CASSIUS. Stoop, then, and wash. How many ages hence
  Shall this our lofty scene be acted over
  In states unborn and accents yet unknown!
BRUTUS. How many times shall Cæsar bleed in sport,
  That now on Pompey's basis lies along[229]
  No worthier than the dust!
CASSIUS. So oft as that shall be,
  So often shall the knot of us be call'd
  The men that gave their country liberty.[230]
DECIUS BRUTUS. What, shall we forth?
CASSIUS. Ay, every man away:
  Brutus shall lead; and we will grace his heels
  With the most boldest[231] and best hearts of Rome.

---

[228] "We all know that we are to die some time; and how long we can draw out our life, is the only thing we concern ourselves about."

[229] So it was in fact: Cæsar fell at the pedestal of Pompey's statue; the statue itself dripping with the blood that spurted from him.

[230] These three speeches, vain-gloriously anticipating the stage celebrity of the deed, are very strange; and, unless there be a shrewd irony lurking in them, I am at a loss to understand the purpose of them. Their effect on my mind has long been to give a very ambitious air to the work of these patriots, and to cast a highly theatrical colour on their alleged virtue.

[231] This doubling of superlatives, as also of comparatives, and of negatives, was common in the Poet's time. So, in The Acts, xxvi. 5, St. Paul says, "after the *most straitest* sect of our religion I lived a Pharisee."

[*Enter a* SERVANT.]

BRUTUS. Soft! Who comes here? A friend of Antony's.
SERVANT. Thus, Brutus, did my master bid me kneel:
   Thus did Mark Antony bid me fall down;
   And, being prostrate, thus he bade me say:
   Brutus is noble, wise, valiant, and honest;
   Cæsar was mighty, bold, royal, and loving:
   Say I love Brutus, and I honour him;
   Say I fear'd Cæsar, honour'd him and loved him.
   If Brutus will vouchsafe that Antony
   May safely come to him, and be resolved[232]
   How Cæsar hath deserved to lie in death,
   Mark Antony shall not love Cæsar dead
   So well as Brutus living; but will follow
   The fortunes and affairs of noble Brutus
   Thorough[233] the hazards of this untrod state
   With all true faith. So says my master Antony.
BRUTUS. Thy master is a wise and valiant Roman;
   I never thought him worse.
   Tell him, so please him come unto this place,
   He shall be satisfied; and, by my honour,
   Depart untouch'd.
SERVANT. I'll fetch him presently. [*Exit.*]
BRUTUS. I know that we shall have him well to friend.
CASSIUS. I wish we may: but yet have I a mind
   That fears him much; and my misgiving still
   Falls shrewdly to the purpose.
BRUTUS. But here comes Antony.

[*Re-enter* ANTONY.]

   Welcome, Mark Antony.
ANTONY. O mighty Cæsar! Dost thou lie so low?
   Are all thy conquests, glories, triumphs, spoils,
   Shrunk to this little measure? Fare thee well.
   I know not, gentlemen, what you intend,
   Who else must be let blood, who else is rank:[234]

---

[232] *Informed, assured, satisfied* are among the old senses of *resolved.*
[233] Shakespeare uses *through* or *thorough* indifferently, as suits his verse. The two are in fact but different forms of the same word.
[234] "Must be let blood" is a mere euphemism for "must be put to death."—"Who else is rank" means "who else has too much blood in him." And the idea is of one who has *overtopped* his equals, and *grown too high* for the public safety.

If I myself, there is no hour so fit
As Cæsar's death hour, nor no instrument
Of half that worth as those your swords, made rich
With the most noble blood of all this world.
I do beseech ye, if you bear me hard,
Now, whilst your purpled hands do reek and smoke,
Fulfil your pleasure. Live a thousand years,[235]
I shall not find myself so apt to die:
No place will please me so, no mean of death,
As here by Cæsar, and by[236] you cut off,
The choice and master spirits of this age.
BRUTUS. O Antony, beg not your death of us.
Though now we must appear bloody and cruel,
As, by our hands and this our present act,
You see we do, yet see you but our hands
And this the bleeding business they have done:
Our hearts you see not; they are pitiful;
And pity to the general wrong of Rome—
As fire drives out fire,[237] so pity pity—
Hath done this deed on Cæsar. For your part,
To you our swords have leaden points, Mark Antony:
Our arms, in strength of malice, and our hearts
Of brothers' temper, do receive you in
With all kind love, good thoughts, and reverence.
CASSIUS. Your voice shall be as strong as any man's
In the disposing of new dignities.[238]
BRUTUS. Only be patient till we have appeased
The multitude, beside themselves with fear,
And then we will deliver you the cause,
Why I, that did love Cæsar when I struck him,
Have thus proceeded.
ANTONY. I doubt not of your wisdom.
Let each man render me his bloody hand:

---

[235] That is, "*if I* live," or "*should* I live, a thousand years."

[236] *By* is here used in two senses; first, in the sense of *near*, or as a sign of place; second, to denote agency, as usual.

[237] Shakespeare uses *fire* as one or two syllables indifferently, to suit his metre. Here the first *fire* is two syllables, the second one.—The allusion is to the old way of salving a burn by holding it up to the fire. So in *Romeo and* Juliet, i. 2: "Tut, man, one fire burns out another's burning; one pain is lessen'd by another's anguish."

[238] This little speech is snugly characteristic. Brutus has been talking about "our hearts," and "kind love, good thoughts, and reverence." To Cassius, all that is mere rose-water humbug, and he knows it is so to Antony too. He therefore hastens to put in such motives as he knows will have weight with Antony, as they also have with himself. And it is somewhat remarkable that several of these patriots, especially Cassius, the two Brutuses, and Trebonius, afterwards accepted the governorship of fat provinces for which they had been prospectively named by Cæsar.

First, Marcus Brutus, will I shake with you;—
Next, Caius Cassius, do I take your hand;—
Now, Decius Brutus, yours;—now yours, Metellus;—
Yours, Cinna; and, my valiant Casca, yours;
Though last, not last in love, yours, good Trebonius.
Gentlemen all,—alas, what shall I say?
My credit now stands on such slippery ground,
That one of two bad ways you must conceit me,[239]
Either a coward or a flatterer.—
That I did love thee, Cæsar, O, 'tis true:
If then thy spirit look upon us now,
Shall it not grieve thee dearer[240] than thy death,
To see thy Anthony making his peace,
Shaking the bloody fingers of thy foes,—
Most noble!—In the presence of thy corpse?
Had I as many eyes as thou hast wounds,
Weeping as fast as they stream forth thy blood,
It would become me better than to close
In terms of friendship with thine enemies.
Pardon me, Julius! Here wast thou bay'd,[241] brave hart;
Here didst thou fall; and here thy hunters stand,
Sign'd in thy spoil, and crimson'd in thy lethe.
O world, thou wast the forest to this hart;
And this, indeed, O world, the heart of thee.
How like a deer, tricken by many princes,
Dost thou here lie!

CASSIUS. Mark Antony,—

ANTONY. Pardon me, Caius Cassius:
The enemies of Cæsar shall say this;
Then, in a friend, it is cold modesty.[242]

CASSIUS. I blame you not for praising Cæsar so;
But what compact mean you to have with us?
Will you be prick'd[243] in number of our friends;
Or shall we on, and not depend on you?

ANTONY. Therefore[244] I took your hands, but was, indeed,
Sway'd from the point, by looking down on Cæsar.

---

[239] Must *conceive of* me, or *construe* me. See page 39, note 133.

[240] Formerly *dear* might signify whatever moved any strong feeling, whether of pleasure or pain. The Poet has many instances of it used as here.

[241] *Bay'd* is *brought to bay*, and so barked at and worried, as a deer by hounds. Shakespeare has the word often in that sense.

[242] *Modesty* in its original sense of *moderation*. Frequent.

[243] *Prick'd* is *marked*. The image is of a list of names written out, and some of them having holes pricked in the paper against them.

[244] *Therefore* is not the illative conjunction here; but means *to that end*, or *for that purpose*.

Friends am I with you all and love you all,
Upon this hope, that you shall give me reasons
Why and wherein Cæsar was dangerous.
BRUTUS. Or else were this a savage spectacle:
Our reasons are so full of good regard
That were you, Antony, the son of Cæsar,
You should be satisfied.
ANTONY. That's all I seek:
And am moreover suitor that I may
Produce his body to the market-place;[245]
And in the pulpit, as becomes a friend,
Speak in the order of his funeral.
BRUTUS. You shall, Mark Antony.
CASSIUS. Brutus, a word with you.
[*Aside to* BRUTUS.] You know not what you do: do not consent
That Antony speak in his funeral:
Know you how much the people may be moved
By that which he will utter?
BRUTUS. [*Aside to* CASSIUS.] By your pardon;
I will myself into the pulpit first,
And show the reason of our Cæsar's death:
What Antony shall speak, I will protest
He speaks by leave and by permission,
And that we are contented Cæsar shall
Have all true rites and lawful ceremonies.
It shall advantage more than do us wrong.
CASSIUS. [*Aside to* BRUTUS.] I know not what may fall; I like it not.
BRUTUS. Mark Antony, here, take you Cæsar's body.
You shall not in your funeral speech blame us,
But speak all good you can devise of Cæsar,
And say you do't by our permission;
Else shall you not have any hand at all
About his funeral: and you shall speak
In the same pulpit whereto I am going,
After my speech is ended.
ANTONY. Be it so.
I do desire no more.
BRUTUS. Prepare the body then, and follow us.

[*Exeunt all but* ANTONY.]

---

[245] *Produce* in the Latin sense of *produco*; implying motion to a place.—Here, and all through this play, *market-place* is the *Forum*, where several rostra were provided for addressing the people. Shakespeare calls these rostra *pulpits.*

ANTONY. O, pardon me, thou bleeding piece of earth,
    That I am meek and gentle with these butchers!
    Thou art the ruins of the noblest man
    That ever lived in the tide of times.
    Woe to the hand that shed this costly blood!
    Over thy wounds now do I prophesy,—
    Which, like dumb mouths, do ope their ruby lips,
    To beg the voice and utterance of my tongue—
    A curse shall light upon the limbs of men;[246]
    Domestic fury and fierce civil strife
    Shall cumber all the parts of Italy;
    Blood and destruction shall be so in use
    And dreadful objects so familiar
    That mothers shall but smile when they behold
    Their infants quarter'd with the hands of war;
    All pity choked[247] with custom of fell deeds:
    And Cæsar's spirit, ranging for revenge,
    With Até[248] by his side come hot from hell,
    Shall in these confines with a monarch's voice
    Cry *Havoc!* and let slip the dogs of war;[249]
    That this foul deed shall smell above the earth
    With carrion men, groaning for burial.

    [*Enter a* SERVANT.]

    You serve Octavius Cæsar, do you not?
SERVANT. I do, Mark Antony.
ANTONY. Cæsar did write for him to come to Rome.
SERVANT. He did receive his letters, and is coming;
    And bid me say to you by word of mouth—
    [*Seeing the body.*] O Cæsar!—
ANTONY. Thy heart is big, get thee apart and weep.
    Passion, I see, is catching; for mine eyes,

---

[246] By *men* Antony means not mankind in general; the scope of the curse being limited by the subsequent words, "the parts of Italy," and "in these confines."—*Limbs* is merely the figure of speech called *Synecdoche*, or the putting of a part of a thing for the whole.

[247] "All pity *being* choked." Ablative absolute again.

[248] Até is the old goddess of discord and mischief. So, in *Much Ado*, ii. 1, Benedick describes Beatrice as "the infernal Ate in good apparel."

[249] *Havoc* was anciently the word of signal for giving no quarter in a battle. It was a high crime for any one to give the signal without authority from the general-in-chief; hence the peculiar force of *monarch's voice*.—To *let slip* a dog was a term of the chase, for releasing the hounds from the leash or *slip* of leather whereby they were held in hand till it was time to let them pursue the animal.—The *dogs of war* are fire, sword, and famine. So in *King Henry V.*, first Chorus: "At his heels, leash'd in like *hounds*, should *famine, sword, and fire*, crouch for employment."

Seeing those beads of sorrow stand in thine,
Began to water. Is thy master coming?
SERVANT. He lies to-night within seven leagues of Rome.
ANTONY. Post back with speed, and tell him what hath chanced:
Here is a mourning Rome, a dangerous Rome,
No Rome of safety for Octavius yet;
Hie hence, and tell him so. Yet, stay awhile;
Thou shalt not back till I have borne this corpse
Into the market-place: there shall I try
In my oration, how the people take
The cruel issue of these bloody men;
According to the which, thou shalt discourse
To young Octavius of the state of things.
Lend me your hand. [*Exeunt with* CÆSAR's *body.*]

SCENE II.

The Same. The Forum.

[*Enter* BRUTUS *and* CASSIUS, *and a throng of* CITIZENS.]

CITIZENS. We will be satisfied; let us be satisfied.
BRUTUS. Then follow me, and give me audience, friends.—
Cassius, go you into the other street,
And part the numbers.—
Those that will hear me speak, let 'em stay here;
Those that will follow Cassius, go with him;
And public reasons shall be rendered
Of Cæsar's death.
FIRST CITIZEN. I will hear Brutus speak.
SECOND CITIZEN. I will hear Cassius; and compare their reasons,
When severally we hear them rendered.

[*Exit* CASSIUS, *with some of the* CITIZENS. BRUTUS *goes into
the rostrum.*]

THIRD CITIZEN. The noble Brutus is ascended: silence!
BRUTUS. Be patient till the last.
Romans, countrymen, and lovers![250] hear me for my cause, and be
silent, that you may hear: believe me for mine honour, and have
respect to mine honour, that you may believe: censure[251] me in

---

[250] *Lover* and *friend* were used as synonymous in the Poet's time. Brutus afterwards
speaks of Cæsar as "my best *lover.*"
[251] *Censure* is here, as often, *judge*; probably used for the jingle it makes with
senses.

your wisdom, and awake your senses, that you may the better judge. If there be any in this assembly, any dear friend of Cæsar's, to him I say, that Brutus' love to Cæsar was no less than his. If then that friend demand why Brutus rose against Cæsar, this is my answer:—Not that I loved Cæsar less, but that I loved Rome more. Had you rather Cæsar were living and die all slaves, than that Cæsar were dead, to live all free men? As Cæsar loved me, I weep for him; as he was fortunate, I rejoice at it; as he was valiant, I honour him: but, as he was ambitious, I slew him. There is tears for his love; joy for his fortune; honour for his valour; and death for his ambition. Who is here so base that would be a bondman? If any, speak; for him have I offended. Who is here so rude that would not be a Roman? If any, speak; for him have I offended. Who is here so vile that will not love his country? If any, speak; for him have I offended. I pause for a reply.

ALL THE CITIZENS. None, Brutus, none.

BRUTUS. Then none have I offended. I have done no more to Cæsar than you shall do to Brutus. The question of his death is enrolled in the Capitol;[252] his glory not extenuated, wherein he was worthy,[253] nor his offences enforced, for which he suffered death.

[*Enter* ANTONY *and others, with* CÆSAR's *body.*]

Here comes his body, mourned by Mark Antony: who, though he had no hand in his death, shall receive the benefit of his dying, a place in the commonwealth; as which of you shall not? With this I depart,—that, as I slew my best lover for the good of Rome, I have the same dagger for myself, when it shall please my country to need my death.[254]

ALL THE CITIZENS. Live, Brutus! live, live!

FIRST CITIZEN. Bring him with triumph home unto his house.

SECOND CITIZEN. Give him a statue with his ancestors.

---

[252] The *reason* of his death is made a matter of solemn official record in the books of the Senate, as showing that the act of killing him was done for public ends, and not from private hate.

[253] His fame is not *lessened* or *whittled down in those points* wherein he was worthy.—*Enforced* is in antithesis to *extenuated*, meaning that his faults are not magnified or forced out of just measure.

[254] In this celebrated speech, which, to my taste, is far from being a model of style either for oratory or any thing else, the Poet seems to have aimed at imitating the manner actually ascribed to Brutus. So, in Plutarch: "They do note that, in some of his Epistles, he counterfeited that briefe compendious manner of speech of the Lacedæmonians." And Shakespeare's idea, as followed out in this speech, is sustained also by the *Dialogus de Oratoribus*, ascribed to Tacitus; wherein it is said that Brutus' style of eloquence was censured as *otiosum et disjunctum*. For, as Verplanck remarks, "the *disjunctum*, the broken-up style, without oratorical continuity, is precisely that assumed by the dramatist."

THIRD CITIZEN. Let him be Cæsar.

FOURTH CITIZEN. Cæsar's better parts
  Shall be crown'd in Brutus.

FIRST CITIZEN. We'll bring him to his house
  With shouts and clamours.

BRUTUS. My countrymen,—

SECOND CITIZEN. Peace, silence! Brutus speaks.

FIRST CITIZEN. Peace, ho!

BRUTUS. Good countrymen, let me depart alone,
  And, for my sake, stay here with Antony:
  Do grace to Cæsar's corpse, and grace his speech
  Tending to Cæsar's glories; which Mark Antony,
  By our permission, is allow'd to make.
  I do entreat you, not a man depart,
  Save I alone, till Antony have spoke. [*Exit.*]

FIRST CITIZEN. Stay, ho! and let us hear Mark Antony.

THIRD CITIZEN. Let him go up into the public chair;
  We'll hear him. Noble Antony, go up.

ANTONY. For Brutus' sake, I am beholding[255] to you. [*Goes up.*]

FOURTH CITIZEN. What does he say of Brutus?

THIRD CITIZEN. He says, for Brutus' sake,
  He finds himself beholding to us all.

FOURTH CITIZEN. 'Twere best he speak no harm of Brutus here.

FIRST CITIZEN. This Cæsar was a tyrant.

THIRD CITIZEN. Nay, that's certain:
  We are blest that Rome is rid of him.

SECOND CITIZEN. Peace! let us hear what Antony can say.

ANTONY. You gentle Romans,—

ALL THE CITIZENS. Peace, ho! let us hear him.

ANTONY. Friends, Romans, countrymen, lend me your ears;
  I come to bury Cæsar, not to praise him.
  The evil that men do lives after them;
  The good is oft interred with their bones;[256]
  So let it be with Cæsar. The noble Brutus
  Hath told you Cæsar was ambitious:[257]
  If it were so, it was a grievous fault,
  And grievously hath Cæsar answer'd it.

---

[255] Shakespeare always uses *beholding*, the active form, for *beholden*, the passive. Here, as elsewhere, it means *obliged*, of course.

[256] We have the same thought in *Henry the Eighth*, iv. 2: "Men's evil manners live in brass; their virtues we write in water."

[257] In Shakespeare's time, the ending *-tious* and various others like it, was often pronounced as two syllables. The same was the case with *-tion*, *-sion*, and divers others. Many instances of the latter have already occurred in this play; as in the preceding scene: "And say you do't by our *permission*."

Here, under leave of Brutus and the rest—
For Brutus is an honourable man;
So are they all, all honourable men—
Come I to speak in Cæsar's funeral.
He was my friend, faithful and just to me:
But Brutus says he was ambitious;
And Brutus is an honourable man.
He hath brought many captives home to Rome
Whose ransoms did the general coffers fill:[258]
Did this in Cæsar seem ambitious?
When that the poor have cried, Cæsar hath wept:
Ambition should be made of sterner stuff:
Yet Brutus says he was ambitious;
And Brutus is an honourable man.
You all did see that on the Lupercal[259]
I thrice presented him a kingly crown,
Which he did thrice refuse: was this ambition?
Yet Brutus says he was ambitious;
And, sure, he is an honourable man.[260]
I speak not to disprove what Brutus spoke,
But here I am to speak what I do know.
You all did love him once, not without cause:
What cause withholds you then, to mourn[261] for him?—
O judgment! thou art fled to brutish beasts,[262]
And men have lost their reason.—Bear with me;
My heart is in the coffin there with Cæsar,
And I must pause till it come back to me.

FIRST CITIZEN. Methinks there is much reason in his sayings.
SECOND CITIZEN. If thou consider rightly of the matter,
    Cæsar has had great wrong.
THIRD CITIZEN. Has he, masters?
    I fear there will a worse come in his place.

---

[258] Cæsar's campaigns in Gaul put vast sums of money into his hands, a large part of which he kept to his own use, as he might have kept it all; but he did also, in fact, make over much of it to the *public treasury*. This was a very popular act, as it lightened the taxation of the city.

[259] That is, on *the day* when the feast of Lupercalia was held.

[260] Of course these repetitions of *honourable man* are intensely ironical; and for that very reason the irony should be studiously kept out of the voice in pronouncing them. I have heard speakers and readers utterly spoil the effect of the speech by specially emphasizing the irony. For, from the extreme delicacy of his position, Antony is obliged to proceed with the utmost caution, until he gets the audience thoroughly in his power. The consummate adroitness which he uses to this end is one of the greatest charms of this incomparable oration.

[261] To *mourn fox from mourning*. Another gerundial infinitive.

[262] *Brutish* is by no means tautological here; the antithetic sense of *human* brutes being most artfully implied.

FOURTH CITIZEN. Mark'd ye his words? He would not take the
  crown;
  Therefore 'tis certain he was not ambitious.
FIRST CITIZEN. If it be found so, some will dear abide it.[263]
SECOND CITIZEN. Poor soul! his eyes are red as fire with weeping.
THIRD CITIZEN. There's not a nobler man in Rome than Antony.
FOURTH CITIZEN. Now mark him, he begins again to speak.
ANTONY. But yesterday the word of Cæsar might
  Have stood against the world; now lies he there.
  And none so poor to do him reverence.[264]
  O masters, if I were disposed to stir
  Your hearts and minds to mutiny and rage,
  I should do Brutus wrong, and Cassius wrong,
  Who, you all know, are honourable men:
  I will not do them wrong; I rather choose
  To wrong the dead, to wrong myself and you,
  Than I will wrong such honourable men.
  But here's a parchment with the seal of Cæsar;
  I found it in his closet, 'tis his will:
  Let but the commons hear this testament,—
  Which, pardon me, I do not mean to read,—
  And they would go and kiss dead Cæsar's wounds
  And dip their napkins[265] in his sacred blood,
  Yea, beg a hair of him for memory,
  And, dying, mention it within their wills,
  Bequeathing it as a rich legacy
  Unto their issue.
FOURTH CITIZEN. We'll hear the will: read it, Mark Antony.
ALL THE CITIZENS. The will, the will! we will hear Cæsar's will.
ANTONY. Have patience, gentle friends, I must not read it;
  It is not meet you know how Cæsar loved you.
  You are not wood, you are not stones, but men;
  And, being men, bearing the will of Cæsar,
  It will inflame you, it will make you mad:
  'Tis good you know not that you are his heirs;
  For, if you should, O, what would come of it!
FOURTH CITIZEN. Read the will; we'll hear it, Antony;
  You shall read us the will,—Cæsar's will.
ANTONY. Will you be patient? will you stay awhile?
  I have o'ershot myself to tell you of it:

[263] Here, again, to *abide* a thing is to *suffer for* it, or, as we now say, to *pay for* it. See page 50, note 227.
[264] And there are none so humble but that he is beneath their reverence, or too low for their regard.
[265] *Napkin* and *handkerchief* were used indifferently.

I fear I wrong the honourable men
Whose daggers have stabb'd Cæsar;[266] I do fear it.
FOURTH CITIZEN. They were traitors: honourable men!
ALL THE CITIZENS. The will! the testament!
SECOND CITIZEN. They were villains, murderers: the will! read the
will.
ANTONY. You will compel me, then, to read the will?
Then make a ring about the corpse of Cæsar,
And let me show you him that made the will.
Shall I descend? and will you give me leave?
SEVERAL CITIZENS. Come down.
SECOND CITIZEN. Descend.
THIRD CITIZEN. You shall have leave. [ANTONY *comes down.*]
FOURTH CITIZEN. A ring; stand round.
FIRST CITIZEN. Stand from the hearse, stand from the body.
SECOND CITIZEN. Room for Antony, most noble Antony.
ANTONY. Nay, press not so upon me; stand far'[267] off.
SEVERAL CITIZENS. Stand back; room; bear back.
ANTONY. If you have tears, prepare to shed them now.
You all do know this mantle: I remember
The first time ever Cæsar put it on;
'Twas on a summer's evening, in his tent,
That day he overcame the Nervii.[268]
Look, in this place ran Cassius' dagger through:
See what a rent the envious[269] Casca made:
Through this the well-beloved Brutus stabb'd;
And as he pluck'd his cursed steel away,
Mark how the blood of Cæsar follow'd it,
As rushing out of doors, to be resolved[270]
If Brutus so unkindly knock'd, or no;

---

[266] Antony now sees that he has the people wholly with him, so that he is perfectly
safe in stabbing the stabbers with these terrible words.—"I have o'ershot myself to tell
you of it" is, "I have gone too far, and hurt my own cause, *in telling* you of it." The
infinitive used gerundively again. We have a like expression in *Henry the Eighth.*, i. 1:
"We may outrun, by violent swiftness, that which we run at, and *lose by over-running*?

[267] The Poet has *far'* for *further* repeatedly.

[268] This is the artfullest and most telling stroke in Antony's speech. The Romans
prided themselves most all upon their military virtue and renown: Cæsar was their
greatest military hero; and his victory over the Nervii was his most noted military exploit.
It occurred during his second campaign in Gaul, in the Summer of the year B.C. 57, and
is narrated with surpassing vividness in the second book of his *Bellum Gallicum.* Of
course the matter about the "mantle" is purely fictitious: Cæsar had on the civic gown,
not the military cloak, when killed; and it was, in fact, the mangled toga that Antony
displayed on this occasion: but the fiction has the effect of making the allusion to the
victory seem perfectly artless and incidental.

[269] *Envious*, again, in its old sense of *malicious* or *malignant.*

[270] *Resolved*, again, for *informed* or *assured.* See page 50, note 232.

For Brutus, as you know, was Cæsar's angel:[271]
Judge, O you gods, how dearly Cæsar loved him!
This was the most unkindest cut of all;
For when the noble Cæsar saw him stab,
Ingratitude, more strong than traitors' arms,
Quite vanquish'd him: then burst his mighty heart;
And, in his mantle muffling up his face,
Even at the base of Pompey's statue,
Which all the while ran blood,[272] great Cæsar fell.
O, what a fall was there, my countrymen!
Then I, and you, and all of us fell down,
Whilst bloody treason flourish'd over us.
O, now you weep; and, I perceive, you feel
The dint of pity:[273] these are gracious drops.
Kind souls, what, weep you when you but behold
Our Cæsar's vesture wounded? Look you here,
Here is himself, marr'd, as you see, with traitors.
FIRST CITIZEN. O piteous spectacle!
SECOND CITIZEN. O noble Cæsar!
THIRD CITIZEN. O woeful day!
FOURTH CITIZEN. O traitors, villains!
FIRST CITIZEN. O most bloody sight!
SECOND CITIZEN. We will be revenged.
ALL THE CITIZENS. Revenge,—about,—seek,—burn,—fire,—
  kill,—slay,—let not a traitor live!
ANTONY. Stay, countrymen.
FIRST CITIZEN. Peace there! hear the noble Antony.
SECOND CITIZEN. We'll hear him, we'll follow him, we'll die with
  him.
ANTONY. Good friends, sweet friends, let me not stir you up
  To such a sudden flood of mutiny.
  They that have done this deed are honourable:
  What private griefs they have, alas, I know not,
  That made them do it: they are wise and honourable,
  And will, no doubt, with reasons answer you.
  I come not, friends, to steal away your hearts:
  I am no orator, as Brutus is;

---

[271] *Angel* here means, apparently, his counterpart, his good genius, or a kind of better and dearer self. See page 42, note 149.

[272] Men report, that Cæsar did still defend himself against the rest, running every way with his body: but when he saw Brutus with his sword drawn in his hand, then he pulled his gown over his head, and made no more resistance, and was driven either casually or purposedly, by the counsel of the conspirators, against the base whereupon Pompey's image stood, which ran all of a gore-blood till he was slain.—PLUTARCH.

[273] *Dint* is, properly, *blow* or *stroke*; here put for the *impression* made by the blow.

But, as you know me all, a plain blunt man,
That love my friend; and that they know full well
That gave me public leave to speak of him:
For I have neither wit,[274] nor words, nor worth,
Action, nor utterance, nor the power of speech,
To stir men's blood: I only speak right on;
I tell you that which you yourselves do know;
Show you sweet Cæsar's wounds, poor poor dumb mouths,
And bid them speak for me: but were I Brutus,
And Brutus Antony, there were an Antony
Would ruffle up your spirits and put a tongue
In every wound of Cæsar that should move
The stones of Rome to rise and mutiny.
ALL THE CITIZENS. We'll mutiny.
FIRST CITIZEN. We'll burn the house of Brutus.
THIRD CITIZEN. Away, then! come, seek the conspirators.
ANTONY. Yet hear me, countrymen; yet hear me speak.
ALL THE CITIZENS. Peace, ho! Hear Antony. Most noble Antony!
ANTONY. Why, friends, you go to do you know not what:
Wherein hath Cæsar thus deserved your loves?
Alas, you know not: I must tell you then:
You have forgot the will I told you of.
ALL THE CITIZENS. Most true. The will! Let's stay and hear the will.
ANTONY. Here is the will, and under Cæsar's seal.
To every Roman citizen he gives,
To every several man, seventy-five drachmas.[275]
SECOND CITIZENS. Most noble Cæsar! We'll revenge his death.
THIRD CITIZEN. O royal Cæsar!
ANTONY. Hear me with patience.
ALL THE CITIZENS. Peace, ho!
ANTONY. Moreover, he hath left you all his walks,
His private arbours and new-planted orchards,
On this side Tiber:[276] he hath left them you,
And to your heirs for ever, common pleasures,
To walk abroad, and recreate yourselves.[277]

---

[274] *Wit* formerly meant *understanding*, and was so used by all writers.

[275] The *drachma* was a Greek coin, equal to 7d. English. In fact, however, Cæsar left to each citizen three hundred sesterces, equivalent to about $14; which was practically as good as at least $100 in our time: no small lift for a poor man.

[276] As this scene lies in the Forum, near the Capitol, Cæsar's gardens are, in fact, on *the other* side Tiber. But the Poet wrote as he read in Plutarch.

[277] When Cæsar's testament was openly read among them, whereby it appeared that he bequeathed unto every citizen of Rome 75 drachmas a man; and that he left his gardens and arbours unto the people, which he had on this side of the river Tiber, in the place where now the temple of Fortune is built; the people then loved him, and were marvellous sorry for him.—PLUTARCH.

Here was a Cæsar! when comes such another?
FIRST CITIZEN. Never, never. Come, away, away!
   We'll burn his body in the holy place,
   And with the brands fire the traitors' houses.
   Take up the body.
SECOND CITIZEN. Go fetch fire.
THIRD CITIZEN. Pluck down benches.
FOURTH CITIZEN. Pluck down forms,[278] windows, any thing.

   [*Exeunt* CITIZENS *with the body.*]

ANTONY. Now let it work. Mischief, thou art afoot,
   Take thou what course thou wilt!

   [*Enter a* SERVANT.]

   How now, fellow!
SERVANT. Sir, Octavius is already come to Rome.
ANTONY. Where is he?
SERVANT. He and Lepidus are at Cæsar's house.
ANTONY. And thither will I straight to visit him:
   He comes upon a wish. Fortune is merry,
   And in this mood will give us any thing.
SERVANT. I heard him say, Brutus and Cassius
   Are rid like madmen through the gates of Rome.
ANTONY. Belike they had some notice of the people,
   How I had moved them. Bring me to Octavius. [*Exeunt.*]

SCENE III.

The Same. A Street.

   [*Enter* CINNA *the poet.*]

CINNA THE POET. I dreamt to-night that I did feast with Cæsar,
   And things unlucky charge my fantasy:[279]
   I have no will to wander forth of doors,
   Yet something leads me forth.

   [*Enter* CITIZENS.]

FIRST CITIZEN. What is your name?

---

[278] A *form* is a long *seat*, like those in an audience-room or a school.
[279] *Unlucky* is *ill-boding* or *portentous. Charge* is *burden* or *oppress.*

SECOND CITIZEN. Whither are you going?

THIRD CITIZEN. Where do you dwell?

FOURTH CITIZEN. Are you a married man or a bachelor?

SECOND CITIZEN. Answer every man directly.

FIRST CITIZEN. Ay, and briefly.

FOURTH CITIZEN. Ay, and wisely.

THIRD CITIZEN. Ay, and truly, you were best.

CINNA THE POET. What is my name? Whither am I going? Where do
I dwell? Am I a married man or a bachelor? Then, to answer every
man directly and briefly, wisely and truly: wisely I say, I am a
bachelor.

SECOND CITIZEN. That's as much as to say, they are fools that
marry: you'll bear me a bang for that,[280] I fear. Proceed; directly.

CINNA THE POET. Directly, I am going to Cæsar's funeral.

FIRST CITIZEN. As a friend or an enemy?

CINNA THE POET. As a friend.

SECOND CITIZEN. That matter is answered directly.

FOURTH CITIZEN. For your dwelling,—briefly.

CINNA THE POET. Briefly, I dwell by the Capitol.

THIRD CITIZEN. Your name, sir, truly.

CINNA THE POET. Truly, my name is Cinna.

FIRST CITIZEN. Tear him to pieces; he's a conspirator.

CINNA THE POET. I am Cinna the poet, I am Cinna the poet.

FOURTH CITIZEN. Tear him for his bad verses, tear him for his bad
verses.

CINNA THE POET. I am not Cinna the conspirator.

FOURTH CITIZEN. It is no matter, his name's Cinna; pluck but his
name out of his heart, and turn him going.[281]

THIRD CITIZEN. Tear him, tear him! Come, brands ho! fire-brands: to
Brutus', to Cassius'; burn all: some to Decius' house, and some to
Casca's; some to Ligarius': away, go!

[*Exeunt.*]

---

[280] "You'll get a banging of me for that."

[281] There was a poet called Cinna, who had been no partaker of the conspiracy but
was always one of Cæsar's chiefest friends: he dreamed, the night before, that Cæsar bad
him to supper with him, and that, he refusing to go, Cæsar was very importunate with
him, and compelled him; so that at length he led him by the hand into a great dark place,
where, being marvellously afraid, he was driven to follow him in spite of his heart. This
dream put him all night into a fever: and yet, notwithstanding, the next morning he went
out of his house, and thrust himself into the press of the common people that were in a
great uproar. And because some one called him by his name Cinna, the people falling
upon him in their rage slew him outright in the market-place.—PLUTARCH.

ACT IV.

SCENE I.

Rome. A Room in ANTONY's *House.*[282]

[ANTONY, OCTAVIUS, *and* LEPIDUS, *seated at a table.*]

ANTONY. These many, then, shall die; their names are prick'd.
OCTAVIUS. Your brother too must die; consent you, Lepidus?[283]
LEPIDUS. I do consent,—
OCTAVIUS. Prick him down, Antony.
LEPIDUS.—Upon condition Publius shall not live,
    Who is your sister's son, Mark Antony.[284]
ANTONY. He shall not live; look, with a spot I damn[285] him.
    But, Lepidus, go you to Cæsar's house;
    Fetch the will hither, and we shall determine
    How to cut off some charge in legacies.
LEPIDUS. What, shall I find you here?
OCTAVIUS. Or here, or at
    The Capitol. [*Exit* LEPIDUS.]
ANTONY. This is a slight unmeritable[286] man,
    Meet to be sent on errands: is it fit,
    The three-fold world divided, he should stand
    One of the three to share it?
OCTAVIUS. So you thought him;
    And took his voice who should be prick'd to die,
    In our black sentence and proscription.

---

[282] The time of this scene was, historically, in November, B.C. 43; some nineteen months after the preceding.—The place of the scene is shown to be at Rome, by Lepidus's being sent to Cæsar's house, and told that he will find his confederates "or here, or at the Capitol." In fact, however, the triumvirs, Octavius, Antonius, and Lepidus, did not meet at Rome to settle the proscription, but on a small island near Bologna.

[283] They could hardly agree whom they would put to death; for every one of them would kill their enemies, and save their kinsmen and friends. Yet, at length, giving place to their greedy desire to be revenged of their enemies, they spurned all reverence of blood and holiness of friendship at their feet. For Cæsar left Cicero to Antonius's will; Antonius also forsook Lucius Cæsar, who was his uncle by his mother; and both of them together suffered Lepidus to kill his own brother Paulus.—PLUTARCH.

[284] According to Plutarch, as quoted in the preceding note, this was *Lucius* Cæsar, not *Publius*; nor was he Antony's *nephew*, but his uncle by the mother's side. A mistake by the Poet, probably.

[285] Both the verb to *damn* and the noun *damnation* were often used in the sense of to *condemn* simply. So it is, properly, in the English Bible.

[286] *Unmeritable* for *unmeriting* or *undeserving.* This indiscriminate use of active and passive forms is very frequent.

ANTONY. Octavius, I have seen more days than you:
    And though we lay these honours on this man,
    To ease ourselves of divers slanderous loads,
    He shall but bear them as the ass bears gold,
    To groan and sweat under the business,
    Either led or driven, as we point the way;
    And having brought our treasure where we will,
    Then take we down his load, and turn him off,
    Like to the empty ass, to shake his ears,
    And graze in commons.[287]
OCTAVIUS. You may do your will;
    But he's a tried and valiant soldier.
ANTONY. So is my horse, Octavius; and for that
    I do appoint him store of provender:
    It is a creature that I teach to fight,
    To wind,[288] to stop, to run directly on,
    His corporal motion govern'd by my spirit.
    And, in some taste, is Lepidus but so;
    He must be taught and train'd and bid go forth;
    A barren-spirited fellow; one that feeds
    On objects, orts and imitations,
    Which, out of use and staled by other men,
    Begin his fashion:[289] do not talk of him,
    But as a property. And now, Octavius,
    Listen great things:—Brutus and Cassius
    Are levying powers: we must straight make head:[290]
    Therefore let our alliance be combined,
    Our best friends made, our means stretch'd
    And let us presently go sit in council,
    How covert matters may be best disclosed,
    And open perils surest answered.
OCTAVIUS. Let us do so: for we are at the stake,
    And bay'd about with many enemies;[291]

---

[287] *Commons*, here, is such pasture-lands as in England were not owned by individuals, but occupied by a given neighbourhood *in common.*

[288] To *wind* is to *turn* or *bend* to the right or the left; the opposite of running "directly on," that is, *straight ahead.*

[289] That is, one who is always interested in, and talking about, such things—books, works of art, &c.—as everybody else has got tired of and thrown aside. So Falstaff's account of Shallow, in *Henry the Fourth, Part 2*, iii. 2: "He came ever in the rearward of the fashion; and sung those tunes to the over-scutch'd huswives which he heard the carmen whistle, and sware they were his Fancies or his Good-nights." In the text, *staled* is *outworn* or *grown stale*; and the reference is not to objects, &c, generally, but only to those which have lost the interest of freshness.

[290] To *make head* is to *raise an army*, or to *lead one forth.* Often so.

[291] An allusion to bear-baiting. One of the old English sports was, to tie a bear to a stake, and then set a pack of dogs to barking at him, and worrying him. So in *Macbeth*, v.

And some that smile have in their hearts, I fear,
Millions of mischiefs. [*Exeunt.*]

SCENE II.

Before BRUTUS's *Tent, in the Camp near Sardis.*[292]

[*Drum. Enter* BRUTUS, LUCILLIUS, TITINIUS, *and Soldiers*;
PINDARUS *meeting them*; LUCIUS *at some distance.*]

BRUTUS. Stand, ho!
LUCILLIUS. Give the word, ho! and stand.
BRUTUS. What now, Lucillius! is Cassius near?
LUCILLIUS. He is at hand; and Pindarus is come
To do you salutation from his master.

[PINDARUS *gives a letter to* BRUTUS.]

BRUTUS. He greets me well. Your master, Pindarus,
In his own change, or by ill officers,[293]
Hath given me some worthy cause to wish
Things done, undone: but, if he be at hand,
I shall be satisfied.
PINDARUS. I do not doubt
But that my noble master will appear
Such as he is, full of regard and honour.
BRUTUS. He is not doubted.—A word, Lucillius;
How he received you, let me be resolved.
LUCILLIUS. With courtesy and with respect enough;
But not with such familiar instances,
Nor with such free and friendly conference,
As he hath used of old.
BRUTUS. Thou hast described
A hot friend cooling: ever note, Lucillius,
When love begins to sicken and decay,
It useth an enforced ceremony.
There are no tricks in plain and simple faith;
But hollow men, like horses hot at hand,[294]

7: "They've tied me to a stake; I cannot fly, but, bear-like, I must fight the course." See, also, page 50, note 241.

[292] This scene is separated from the foregoing, historically, by about a year; the remaining events of the drama having taken place in the Fall, B.C. 42.

[293] That is, either by his own command, or by officers, subordinates, who have abused their trust, prostituting it to the ends of private gain.

[294] Horses spirited or mettlesome when held back, or restrained.

Make gallant show and promise of their mettle;
But when they should endure the bloody spur,
They fall their crests, and, like deceitful jades,[295]
Sink in the trial. Comes his army on?

LUCILLIUS. They mean this night in Sardis to be quarter'd;
The greater part, the horse in general,
Are come with Cassius. [*March within.*]

BRUTUS. Hark! he is arrived:
March gently on to meet him.

[*Enter* CASSIUS *and* SOLDIERS.]

CASSIUS. Stand, ho!

BRUTUS. Stand, ho! Speak the word along.

FIRST SOLDIER. Stand!

SECOND SOLDIER. Stand!

THIRD SOLDIER. Stand!

CASSIUS. Most noble brother, you have done me wrong.

BRUTUS. Judge me, you gods! wrong I mine enemies?
And, if not so, how should I wrong a brother?

CASSIUS. Brutus, this sober form of yours hides wrongs;
And when you do them—

BRUTUS. Cassius, be content.
Speak your griefs softly: I do know you well.
Before the eyes of both our armies here,
Which should perceive nothing but love from us,
Let us not wrangle: bid them move away;
Then in my tent, Cassius, enlarge[296] your griefs,
And I will give you audience.

CASSIUS. Pindarus,
Bid our commanders lead their charges[297] off
A little from this ground.

BRUTUS. Lucillius, do you the like; and let no man
Come to our tent till we have done our conference.
Let Lucius and Titinius guard our door. [*Exeunt.*]

---

[295] Here, as often, *fall* is transitive; *let fall.*—A deceitful jade is a horse that promises well in appearance, but "sinks in the trial."

[296] To *enlarge* is, properly, to *set free* or to *let go at large*; here it means *speak freely of* or *unfold.*

[297] "Their *charges*" are, of course, the *troops* under their command.

SCENE III.

Within the Tent of BRUTUS.

[*Enter* BRUTUS *and* CASSIUS.]

CASSIUS. That you have wrong'd me doth appear in this:
You have condemn'd and noted[298] Lucius Pella
For taking bribes here of the Sardians;
Wherein my letters, praying on his side,
Because I knew the man, were slighted off.
BRUTUS. You wronged yourself to write[299] in such a case.
CASSIUS. In such a time as this it is not meet
That every nice offence should bear his[300] comment.
BRUTUS. Let me tell you, Cassius, you yourself
Are much condemn'd to have an itching palm;
To sell and mart your offices for gold
To undeservers.
CASSIUS. I an itching palm!
You know that you are Brutus that speak this,
Or, by the gods, this speech were else your last.
BRUTUS. The name of Cassius honours this corruption,
And chastisement doth therefore hide his head.
CASSIUS. Chastisement!
BRUTUS. Remember March, the Ides of March remember:
Did not great Julius bleed for justice' sake?
What villain touch'd his body, that did stab,
And not for justice? What, shall one of us
That struck the foremost man of all this world
But for supporting robbers,—shall we now
Contaminate our fingers with base bribes,
And sell the mighty space of our large honours
For so much trash as may be grasped thus?
I had rather be a dog, and bay the moon,

---

[298] That is, *disgraced* him, set a mark or stigma upon him.
[299] "Wrong'd yourself *by writing*." The infinitive used gerundively again. So too in the second speech after, "condemn'd *to have*" is condemn'd *for having*, also "*to sell* and mart," *for selling* and *marting*. The usage is uncommonly frequent in this play.
[300] *His* for *its*, as usual, referring to *offence*. The meaning is that every *petty* or *trifling* offence should not be rigidly scrutinized and censured. *Nice* was often used thus.—Cassius naturally thinks that "the honourable men whose daggers have stabb'd Cæsar" should not peril their cause by moral squeamishness. And it is a very noteworthy point, that the digesting of that act seems to have entailed upon Brutus a sort of moral dyspepsia. It appears, a little further on, that he is more willing to receive and apply money got by others than to use the necessary means of getting it.

Than such a Roman.

CASSIUS. Brutus, bay not me;
I'll not endure it: you forget yourself,
To hedge me in;[301] I am a soldier, I,
Older in practise, abler than yourself
To make conditions.[302]

BRUTUS. Go to;[303] you are not, Cassius.

CASSIUS. I am.

BRUTUS. I say you are not.

CASSIUS. Urge me no more, I shall forget myself;
Have mind upon your health, tempt me no further.

BRUTUS. Away, slight man!

CASSIUS. Is't possible?

BRUTUS. Hear me, for I will speak.
Must I give way and room to your rash choler?
Shall I be frighted when a madman stares?

CASSIUS. O ye gods, ye gods! must I endure all this?

BRUTUS. All this! ay, more: fret till your proud heart break;
Go show your slaves how choleric you are,
And make your bondmen tremble. Must I budge?
Must I observe you? must I stand and crouch
Under your testy humour? By the gods
You shall digest the venom of your spleen,[304]
Though it do split you; for, from this day forth,
I'll use you for my mirth, yea, for my laughter,
When you are waspish.

CASSIUS. Is it come to this?

BRUTUS. You say you are a better soldier:
Let it appear so; make your vaunting true,
And it shall please me well: for mine own part,
I shall be glad to learn of noble men.

CASSIUS. You wrong me every way; you wrong me, Brutus;
I said, an elder soldier, not a better:[305]

---

[301] Still another gerundial infinitive: "*In hedging* me in."

[302] Now Cassius would have done Brutus much honour, as Brutus did unto him, but Brutus most commonly prevented him, and went first unto him, both because he was the elder man as also for that he was sickly of body. And men reputed him commonly to be very skilful in wars, but otherwise marvellous choleric and cruel, who sought to rule men by fear rather than with lenity.—PLUTARCH.

[303] *Go to* is a phrase of varying import, sometimes of reproof, sometimes of encouragement. *Hush up, come on, go ahead, be off* are among its meanings. It was used a great deal, especially in colloquial speech.

[304] The spleen was held to be the special seat of the sudden and explosive emotions and passions, whether of mirth or anger.

[305] This mistake of Brutus is well conceived. Cassius was much the abler soldier, and Brutus knew it; and the mistake grew from his consciousness of the truth of what he thought he heard. Long before this time, Cassius had served as Quaestor under Marcus

Did I say *better*?

BRUTUS. If you did, I care not.

CASSIUS. When Cæsar lived, he durst not thus have moved me.

BRUTUS. Peace, peace! you durst not so have tempted him.

CASSIUS. I durst not!

BRUTUS. No.

CASSIUS. What, durst not tempt him!

BRUTUS. For your life you durst not!

CASSIUS. Do not presume too much upon my love;
   I may do that I shall be sorry for.

BRUTUS. You have done that you should be sorry for.
   There is no terror, Cassius, in your threats,
   For I am arm'd so strong in honesty
   That they pass by me as the idle wind,
   Which I respect not. I did send to you
   For certain sums of gold, which you denied me;—
   For I can raise no money by vile means:
   By heaven, I had rather coin my heart,
   And drop my blood for drachmas, than to wring
   From the hard hands of peasants their vile trash
   By any indirection:[306]—I did send
   To you for gold to pay my legions,
   Which you denied me: was that done like Cassius?
   Should I have answer'd Caius Cassius so?
   When Marcus Brutus grows so covetous,
   To lock such rascal counters[307] from his friends,
   Be ready, gods, with all your thunderbolts;
   Dash him to pieces!

CASSIUS. I denied you not.[308]

BRUTUS. You did.

CASSIUS. I did not: he was but a fool that brought

Crassus in his expedition against the Parthians; and, when the army was torn all to pieces, both Crassus and his son being killed, Cassius displayed great ability in bringing off a remnant; as he also did after that, in the military administration of Syria.

[306] *Indirection* is, properly, *crookedness.* As the Latin *directus* is *straight,* hence *right,* so *indirectus* is *crooked,* hence *wrong.*

[307] "So covetous *as* to lock," of course. The Poet often omits *as* in such cases, for prosodical reasons.—*Rascal* was much used as a general term of contempt, meaning *worthless* or *base.*—*Counters* were round pieces of cheap metal used in making calculations.

[308] Whilst Brutus and Cassius were together in the city of Smyrna, Brutus prayed Cassius to let him have part of the money whereof he had great store. Cassius's friends hindered this request, and earnestly dissuaded him from it; persuading him, that it was no reason that Brutus should have the money which Cassius had gotten together by sparing, and levied with great evil will of the people their subjects, for him to bestow liberally upon his soldiers, and by this means to win their good wills, by Cassius's charge. Notwithstanding, Cassius gave him the third part of this total sum.—PLUTARCH.

My answer back. Brutus hath rived my heart:
A friend should bear his friend's infirmities,
But Brutus makes mine greater than they are.

BRUTUS. I do not, till you practise them on me.

CASSIUS. You love me not.

BRUTUS. I do not like your faults.

CASSIUS. A friendly eye could never see such faults.

BRUTUS. A flatterer's would not, though they do appear
As huge as high Olympus.

CASSIUS. Come, Antony, and young Octavius, come,
Revenge yourselves alone on Cassius,
For Cassius is aweary of the world;
Hated by one he loves; braved[309] by his brother;
Cheque'd like a bondman; all his faults observed,
Set in a note-book, learn'd, and conn'd by rote,
To cast into my teeth. O, I could weep
My spirit from mine eyes!—There is my dagger,
And here my naked breast; within, a heart
Dearer than Plutus' mine,[310] richer than gold:
If that thou be'st a Roman, take it forth;
I, that denied thee gold, will give my heart:
Strike, as thou didst at Cæsar; for, I know,
When thou didst hate him worst, thou lovedst him better
Than ever thou lovedst Cassius.

BRUTUS. Sheathe your dagger:
Be angry when you will, it shall have scope;
Do what you will, dishonour shall be humour.[311]
O Cassius, you are yoked with a lamb
That carries anger as the flint bears fire;[312]
Who, much enforced, shows a hasty spark,
And straight is cold again.

CASSIUS. Hath Cassius lived
To be but mirth and laughter to his Brutus,
When grief, and blood ill-temper'd, vexeth him?

BRUTUS. When I spoke that, I was ill-temper'd too.

---

[309] *Braved* is *defied*, or treated with *bluster* and *bravado.*

[310] Plutus is the old god of riches, who had all the world's gold in his keeping and disposal.

[311] "Whatever dishonourable thing you may do, I will set it down to the humour or infirmity of the moment."

[312] In my boyhood, the idea was common, of fire *sleeping* in the flint, and being awaked by the stroke of the steel. I am not sure whether it was known in the Poet's time, that in fact the flint cuts off microscopic bits of steel, which are ignited by the friction. Hooker takes it as Shakespeare does; *Ecclesiastical Polity*, vii. 22, 3: "It is not sufficient to carry religion in our hearts, as *fire is carried in flint-stones*, but we are outwardly, visibly, apparently, to serve and honour the living God."

CASSIUS. Do you confess so much? Give me your hand.
BRUTUS. And my heart too.

[*They embrace.*]

CASSIUS. O Brutus,—
BRUTUS. What's the matter?
CASSIUS. Have not you love enough to bear with me,
    When that rash humour which my mother gave me
    Makes me forgetful?
BRUTUS. Yes, Cassius; and, from henceforth,
    When you are over-earnest with your Brutus,
    He'll think your mother chides, and leave you so.
POET. [*Within.*] Let me go in to see the generals;
    There is some grudge between 'em, 'tis not meet
    They be alone.
LUCILLIUS. [*Within.*] You shall not come to them.
POET. [*Within.*] Nothing but death shall stay me.

[*Enter* POET, *followed by* LUCILLIUS, TITINIUS, *and*
    LUCIUS.]

CASSIUS. How now! what's the matter?
POET. For shame, you generals! what do you mean?
    Love, and be friends, as two such men should be;
    For I have seen more years, I'm sure, than ye.[313]
CASSIUS. Ha, ha! how vilely doth this cynic rhyme!
BRUTUS. Get you hence, sirrah; saucy fellow, hence!
CASSIUS. Bear with him, Brutus; 'tis his fashion.
BRUTUS. I'll know his humour, when he knows his time:
    What should the wars do with these jigging fools?
    Companion, hence![314]

---

[313] One Marcus Favonius, that took upon him to counterfeit a philosopher, not with wisdom and discretion, but with a certain bedlam and frantic motion, would needs come into the chamber, though the men offered to keep him out. Now, though he used this bold manner of speech after the profession of the Cynic philosophers, (as who would say, Dogs,) yet his boldness did not hurt many times, because they did but laugh at him to see him so mad. This Favonius at that time, in despite of the door-keepers, came into the chamber, and with a certain scoffing and mocking gesture, which he counterfeited of purpose, rehearsed the verses which old Nestor said in Homer:

    My lords, I pray you hearken both to me,
    For I have seen mo years than suchie three.

Cassius fell a-laughing at him; but Brutus thrust him out of the chamber, and called him dog, and counterfeit Cynic. Howbeit his coming in brake their strife at that time, and so they left each other.—PLUTARCH.

CASSIUS. Away, away, be gone. [*Exit* POET.]

BRUTUS. Lucillius and Titinius, bid the commanders
    Prepare to lodge their companies to-night.

CASSIUS. And come yourselves, and bring Messala with you
    Immediately to us. [*Exeunt* LUCILLIUS *and* TITINIUS.]

BRUTUS. Lucius, a bowl of wine!

CASSIUS. I did not think you could have been so angry.

BRUTUS. O Cassius, I am sick of many griefs.

CASSIUS. Of your philosophy you make no use,
    If you give place to accidental evils.[315]

BRUTUS. No man bears sorrow better. Portia is dead.

CASSIUS. Ha! Portia!

BRUTUS. She is dead.

CASSIUS. How 'scaped I killing when I cross'd you so!—
    O insupportable and touching loss!—
    Upon what sickness?

BRUTUS. Impatient[316] of my absence,
    And grief that young Octavius with Mark Antony
    Have made themselves so strong;—for with her death
    That tidings came;—with this she fell distraught,
    And, her attendants absent, swallow'd fire.[317]

CASSIUS. And died so?

BRUTUS. Even so.

CASSIUS. O ye immortal gods!

[*Enter* LUCIUS, *with wine and taper.*]

BRUTUS. Speak no more of her. Give me a bowl of wine.
    In this I bury all unkindness, Cassius. [*Drinks.*]

---

[314] *Jig* signified a ballad or ditty, as well as a dance. *Companion* is here a term of contempt, as we now *use fellow.*

[315] In his philosophy, Brutus was a mixture of the Stoic and the Platonist. What he says of Portia's death is among the best things in the play, and is in Shakespeare's noblest style. Deep grief loves not many words.

[316] Strict harmony of construction would require *impatience* here, or else *grieved* for *grief* in the next line. But the Poet is not very particular in such matters. The sense is clear enough.

[317] *Distract* for *distracted.* The shortening of preterites in this way was very common.—It appears something uncertain whether Portia's death was before or after her husband's. Plutarch represents it as occurring before; but Merivale follows those who place it after. Plutarch's account is as follows: "For Portia, Brutus's wife, Nicolaus the philosopher and Valerius Maximus do write, that she determining to kill herself (her friends carefully looking to her to keep her from it) took hot burning coals, and cast them into her mouth, and kept her mouth so close that she choked herself. There was a letter of Brutus found, written to his friends, complaining of their negligence, that, his wife being sick, they would not help her, but suffered her to kill herself, choosing to die rather than to languish in pain."

CASSIUS. My heart is thirsty for that noble pledge.—
    Fill, Lucius, till the wine o'erswell the cup;
    I cannot drink too much of Brutus' love. [*Drinks.*]
BRUTUS. Come in, Titinius!—[*Exit* LUCIUS.]

    [*Re-enter* TITINIUS, *with* MESSALA.]

    Welcome, good Messala.—
    Now sit we close about this taper here,
    And call in question[318] our necessities.
CASSIUS. Portia, art thou gone?
BRUTUS. No more, I pray you.—
    Messala, I have here received letters,
    That young Octavius and Mark Antony
    Come down upon us with a mighty power,
    Bending their expedition[319] toward Philippi.
MESSALA. Myself have letters of the selfsame tenor.
BRUTUS. With what addition?
MESSALA. That by proscription and bills of outlawry,
    Octavius, Antony, and Lepidus,
    Have put to death an hundred senators.
BRUTUS. Therein our letters do not well agree;
    Mine speak of seventy senators that died
    By their proscriptions, Cicero being one.[320]
CASSIUS. Cicero one!
MESSALA. Cicero is dead,
    And by that order of proscription.—
    Had you your letters from your wife, my lord?
BRUTUS. No, Messala.
MESSALA. Nor nothing in your letters writ of her?
BRUTUS. Nothing, Messala.[321]
MESSALA. That, methinks, is strange.
BRUTUS. Why ask you? Hear you aught of her in yours?
MESSALA. No, my lord.
BRUTUS. Now, as you are a Roman, tell me true.

---

[318] "Call in *question*" here means *talk* or *converse about. Question,* both noun and verb, was often used in that sense.

[319] *Directing* their *march.* So the Poet has *expedition* repeatedly.

[320] These three, Octavius, Antonius, and Lepidus, made an agreement, and divided the provinces belonging to the empire of Rome among themselves, and did set up bills of proscription and outlawry, condemning two hundred of the noblest men of Rome to suffer death, and among that number Cicero was one.—PLUTARCH.

[321] This may seem inconsistent with what has gone before: but we are to suppose that Brutus's friends at Rome did not write to him directly of Portia's death, lest the news might upset him too much; but wrote to some common friends in the army, directing them to break the news to him, as they should deem it safe and prudent to do so.

MESSALA. Then like a Roman bear the truth I tell:
  For certain she is dead, and by strange manner.
BRUTUS. Why, farewell, Portia.—We must die, Messala:
  With meditating that she must die once,[322]
  I have the patience to endure it now.
MESSALA. Even so great men great losses should endure.
CASSIUS. I have as much of this in art[323] as you,
  But yet my nature could not bear it so.
BRUTUS. Well, to our work alive.[324] What do you think
  Of marching to Philippi presently?
CASSIUS. I do not think it good.
BRUTUS. Your reason?
CASSIUS. This it is:
  'Tis better that the enemy seek us:
  So shall he waste his means, weary his soldiers,
  Doing himself offence; whilst we, lying still,
  Are full of rest, defense, and nimbleness.
BRUTUS. Good reasons must, of force,[325] give place to better.
  The people 'twixt Philippi and this ground
  Do stand but in a forced affection;
  For they have grudged us contribution:
  The enemy, marching along by them,
  By them shall make a fuller number up,
  Come on refresh'd, new-added, and encouraged;
  From which advantage shall we cut him off,
  If at Philippi we do face him there,
  These people at our back.
CASSIUS. Hear me, good brother.
BRUTUS. Under your pardon. You must note beside,
  That we have tried the utmost of our friends,
  Our legions are brim-full, our cause is ripe:
  The enemy increaseth every day;
  We, at the height, are ready to decline.
  There is a tide in the affairs of men,
  Which, taken at the flood, leads on to fortune;

---

[322] *Once* for *one time or other, sometime.* So in *The Merry Wives*, iii. 4: "I pray thee, *once* to-night give my sweet Nan this ring."

[323] *Art* was sometimes used for *theory* as opposed to *practice.*

[324] Probably meaning "the work we have to do *with the living.*"

[325] *Of force* is of *necessity* or *necessarily.*—Plutarch represents this talk as occurring at Philippi just before the battle: "Cassius was of opinion not to try this war at one battle, but rather to delay time, and to draw it out in length, considering that they were the stronger in money, and the weaker in men and armour. But Brutus, in contrary manner, did always, before and at that time also, desire nothing more than to put all to the hazard of battle, as soon as might be possible; to the end he might either quickly restore his country to her liberty, or rid him of this miserable world."

Omitted, all the voyage of their life
Is bound in shallows and in miseries.
On such a full sea are we now afloat;
And we must take the current when it serves,
Or lose our ventures.[326]

CASSIUS. Then, with your will, go on;
  We'll along ourselves, and meet them at Philippi.
BRUTUS. The deep of night is crept upon our talk,
  And nature must obey necessity;
  Which we will niggard with a little rest.
  There is no more to say?
CASSIUS. No more. Good night:
  Early to-morrow will we rise, and hence.
BRUTUS. Lucius, my gown!—Farewell, good Messala:—
  Good night, Titinius:—noble, noble Cassius,
  Good night, and good repose.
CASSIUS. O my dear brother!
  This was an ill beginning of the night:
  Never come such division 'tween our souls!
  Let it not, Brutus.
BRUTUS. Every thing is well.
CASSIUS. Good night, my lord.
BRUTUS. Good night, good brother.
TITINIUS *and* MESSALA. Good night, Lord Brutus.
BRUTUS. Farewell, every one.—

[*Exeunt* CASSIUS, TITINIUS *and* MESSALA.]

[*Re-enter* LUCIUS, *with the gown.*]

Give me the gown. Where is thy instrument?
LUCIUS. Here in the tent.
BRUTUS. What, thou speak'st drowsily?
  Poor knave,[327] I blame thee not; thou art o'er-watch'd.
  Call Claudius and some other of my men:
  I'll have them sleep on cushions in my tent.
LUCIUS. Varrus and Claudius!

[*Enter* VARRUS *and* CLAUDIUS.]

VARRUS. Calls my lord?

---

[326] *Ventures* for what is *risked* or *adventured*. The figure of a ship is kept up; and *venture* denotes whatever is put on board, in hope of profit. The Poet has it repeatedly so.
[327] *Knave* was much used as a term of endearment, or of loving familiarity with those of lower rank.

BRUTUS. I pray you, sirs, lie in my tent and sleep;
    It may be I shall raise you by and by
    On business to my brother Cassius.
VARRUS. So please you, we will stand and watch your pleasure.
BRUTUS. I will not have it so: lie down, good sirs;
    It may be I shall otherwise bethink me.—
    Look, Lucius, here's the book I sought for so;
    I put it in the pocket of my gown.[328]

      [VARRUS *and* CLAUDIUS *lie down.*]

LUCIUS. I was sure your lordship did not give it me.
BRUTUS. Bear with me, good boy, I am much forgetful.
    Canst thou hold up thy heavy eyes awhile,
    And touch thy instrument a strain or two?
LUCIUS. Ay, my lord, an't please you.
BRUTUS. It does, my boy:
    I trouble thee too much, but thou art willing.
LUCIUS. It is my duty, sir.
BRUTUS. I should not urge thy duty past thy might;
    I know young bloods[329] look for a time of rest.
LUCIUS. I have slept, my lord, already.
BRUTUS. It was well done; and thou shalt sleep again;
    I will not hold thee long: if I do live,
    I will be good to thee.—

      [LUCIUS *plays and sings till he falls asleep.*]

    This is a sleepy tune.—O murderous slumber,
    Lay'st thou thy leaden mace upon my boy,
    That plays thee music?[330]—Gentle knave, good night;
    I will not do thee so much wrong to wake thee:
    If thou dost nod, thou break'st thy instrument;
    I'll take it from thee; and, good boy, good night.—

---

[328] These two simple lines are among the best things in the play. Just consider how much is implied in them, and what a picture they give of the earnest, thoughtful, book-loving Brutus. And indeed all his noblest traits of character come out, "in simple and pure soul," in this exquisite scene with Lucius, which is hardly surpassed by anything in Shakespeare.

[329] *Bloods* for *persons.* So in *Much Ado*, iii. 3: "How giddily he turns about all the hot bloods between fourteen and five-and-thirty."

[330] *Mace* was formerly used for *sceptre.* The mace is called *leaden*, from its causing heaviness in the subject of it.—Slumber has the epithet *murderous*, because sleep is regarded as the image of death; or, as Shelley puts it, "Death and his brother Sleep."— The boy is spoken of as playing music to Slumber, because the purpose of his music is to soothe the perturbations out of his master's mind, and put him to sleep.

Let me see, let me see; is not the leaf turn'd down
Where I left reading? Here it is, I think.

[*Enter the Ghost of* CÆSAR.]

How ill this taper burns![331]—Ha! Who comes here?
I think it is the weakness of mine eyes
That shapes this monstrous apparition.
It comes upon me.—Art thou any thing?
Art thou some god, some angel, or some devil,
That makest my blood cold and my hair to stare?[332]
Speak to me what thou art.
GHOST. Thy evil spirit, Brutus.
BRUTUS. Why comest thou?
GHOST. To tell thee thou shalt see me at Philippi.
BRUTUS. Well; then I shall see thee again?
GHOST. Ay, at Philippi.
BRUTUS. Why, I will see thee at Philippi, then. [*Exit Ghost.*]
Now I have taken heart thou vanishest:[333]
Ill spirit, I would hold more talk with thee.[334]—
Boy, Lucius!—Varrus! Claudius! Sirs, awake!—
Claudius!
LUCIUS. The strings, my lord, are false.
BRUTUS. He thinks he still is at his instrument.—
Lucius, awake!
LUCIUS. My lord?
BRUTUS. Didst thou dream, Lucius, that thou so criedst out?
LUCIUS. My lord, I do not know that I did cry.

---

[331] The coming of a ghost was believed to make lights burn dimly. So, in *Richard the Third*, v. 3, when the ghosts appear to Richard, he says, "The lights *burn blue.*"

[332] A singular use of *stare*. Of course it must mean to *stick out*, or, as it is in *Hamlet*, to "*stand on end*, like quills upon the fretful porpentine." We have a similar expression in *The Tempest*, i. 2: "Ferdinand, with hair *upstaring,*—then like reeds, not hair."

[333] This strongly, though quietly, marks the Ghost as *subjective*: as soon as Brutus recovers his firmness, the illusion is broken. The order of things is highly judicious here, in bringing the "horrible vision" upon Brutus just after he has heard of Portia's shocking death. With that great sorrow weighing upon him, he might well see ghosts. The thickening of calamities upon him, growing out of his stabbing exploit, naturally awakens remorse.

[334] Above all, the ghost that appeared unto Brutus shewed plainly that the gods were offended with the murder of Cæsar. The vision was thus: Brutus thought he heard a noise at his tent-door, and, looking towards the light of the lamp that waxed very dim, he saw a horrible vision of a man, of a wonderful greatness and dreadful look, which at the first made him marvellously afraid. But when he saw that it did no hurt, but stood at his bedside and said nothing; at length he asked him what he was. The image answered him: "I am thy ill angel, Brutus, and thou shalt see me by the city of Philippes." Then Brutus replied again, and said, "Well, I shall see thee then." Therewithal the spirit presently vanished from him.—PLUTARCH.

BRUTUS. Yes, that thou didst: didst thou see any thing?
LUCIUS. Nothing, my lord.
BRUTUS. Sleep again, Lucius.—Sirrah Claudius!—
  Fellow thou, awake!
VARRUS. My lord?
CLAUDIUS. My lord?
BRUTUS. Why did you so cry out, sirs, in your sleep?
VARRUS and CLAUDIUS. Did we, my lord?
BRUTUS. Ay: saw you any thing?
VARRUS. No, my lord, I saw nothing.
CLAUDIUS. Nor I, my lord.
BRUTUS. Go and commend me to my brother Cassius;
  Bid him set on his powers betimes before,
  And we will follow.
VARRUS and CLAUDIUS. It shall be done, my lord. [*Exeunt.*]

ACT V.

SCENE I.

The Plains of Philippi.

[*Enter* OCTAVIUS, ANTONY, *and their* Army.]

OCTAVIUS. Now, Antony, our hopes are answered:
  You said the enemy would not come down,
  But keep the hills and upper regions;
  It proves not so: their battles[335] are at hand;
  They mean to warn[336] us at Philippi here,
  Answering before we do demand of them.
ANTONY. Tut, I am in their bosoms, and I know
  Wherefore they do it: they could[337] be content
  To visit other places; and come down
  With fearful bravery,[338] thinking by this face
  To fasten in our thoughts that they have courage;
  But 'tis not so.

---

[335] *Battle* was used for an *army*, especially an army *embattled*, or ordered in battle-array. The plural is here used with historical correctness, as Brutus and Cassius had each an army; the two armies of course co-operating, and acting together as one.

[336] To *warn* for to *summon*. So in *King John*: "Who is it that hath *warn'd* us to the walls?" And in *King Richard III.*: "And sent to *warn* them to his royal presence."

[337] *Could* for *would*. The auxiliaries *could*, *should*, and *would* were often used indiscriminately.—*Content*, here, means more than in our use, and has the sense *of be glad*, or *prefer*.

[338] *Bravery* is *bravado* or *defiance*. Often so. The epithet *fearful* probably means that fear is what thus puts them upon attempting to intimidate by display and brag.

[*Enter a* MESSENGER.]

MESSENGER. Prepare you, generals:
   The enemy comes on in gallant show;
   Their bloody sign of battle is hung out,
   And something to be done immediately.
ANTONY. Octavius, lead your battle softly on,
   Upon the left hand of the even field.
OCTAVIUS. Upon the right hand I; keep thou the left.
ANTONY. Why do you cross me in this exigent?
OCTAVIUS. I do not cross you; but I will do so.[339] [*March.*]

   [*Drum.* Enter BRUTUS, CASSIUS, *and their* ARMY;
      LUCILLIUS, TITINIUS, MESSALA, *and others.*]

BRUTUS. They stand, and would have parley.
CASSIUS. Stand fast, Titinius: we must out and talk.
OCTAVIUS. Mark Antony, shall we give sign of battle?
ANTONY. No, Cæsar, we will answer on their charge.[340]
   Make forth; the generals would have some words.
OCTAVIUS. Stir not until the signal.

   [ANTONY *and* OCTAVIUS *meet* BRUTUS *and* CASSIUS.]

BRUTUS. Words before blows: is it so, countrymen?
OCTAVIUS. Not that we love words better, as you do.
BRUTUS. Good words are better than bad strokes, Octavius.
ANTONY. In your bad strokes, Brutus, you give good words:
   Witness the hole you made in Cæsar's heart,
   Crying, *Long live! hail, Cæsar!*
CASSIUS. Antony,
   The posture of your blows are yet unknown;[341]

---

[339] That is, "I will do as I have said"; not, "I will cross you." At this time, Octavius was but twenty-one years old, and Antony was old enough to be his father. At the time of Cæsar's death, when Octavius was in his nineteenth year, Antony thought he was going to manage him easily and have it all his own way with him, but he found the youngster as stiff as a crowbar, and could do nothing with him. Cæsar's youngest sister Julia was married to Marcus Atius Balbus, and their daughter Atia, again, was married to Caius Octavius, a nobleman of the Plebeian order. From this marriage sprang the present Octavius, who afterwards became the Emperor Augustus. He was mainly educated by his great-uncle, was advanced to the Patrician order, and was adopted as his son and heir; so that his full and proper designation at this time was Caius Julius Cæsar Octavianus. The text gives a right taste of the man, who always stood firm as a post against Antony, till the latter finally knocked himself to pieces against him.
   [340] *Charge* for *attack*; and *answer* in the sense of *meet in combat.*
   [341] *Posture* for *nature* or *manner*, probably; rather an odd use of the word.—The

But for your words, they rob the Hybla bees,
And leave them honeyless.[342]

ANTONY. Not stingless too.

BRUTUS. O, yes, and soundless too;
For you have stol'n their buzzing, Antony,
And very wisely threat before you sting.

ANTONY. Villains, you did not so, when your vile daggers
Hack'd one another in the sides of Cæsar:
You show'd your teeth like apes, and fawn'd like hounds,
And bow'd like bondmen, kissing Cæsar's feet;
Whilst damned Casca, like a cur, behind
Struck Cæsar on the neck. O you flatterers!

CASSIUS. Flatterers! Now, Brutus, thank yourself:
This tongue had not offended so to-day,
If Cassius might have ruled.

OCTAVIUS. Come, come, the cause: if arguing make us sweat,
The proof of it will turn to redder drops.
Look,—
I draw a sword against conspirators;
When think you that the sword goes up again?
Never, till Cæsar's three and thirty wounds
Be well avenged;[343] or till another Cæsar
Have added slaughter to the sword of traitors.[344]

BRUTUS. Cæsar, thou canst not die by traitors' hands,
Unless thou bring'st them with thee.

OCTAVIUS. So I hope;
I was not born to die on Brutus' sword.

BRUTUS. O, if thou wert the noblest of thy strain,[345]
Young man, thou couldst not die more honourable.

---

verb *are* is made to agree with the nearest substantive, *blows*, instead of with its proper nominative, *posture*.

[342] *Hybla* was the name of a place in Sicily, noted for the fine flavour of its honey.—The meaning is, that Antony could not be so "honey-tongued," unless he had quite exhausted thyme-flavoured Hybla.

[343] The historical number of Cæsar's wounds is three-and-*twenty*, and so Shakespeare read it in Plutarch. But the poets care little for exactness in such matters. In Beaumont and Fletcher's *Two Noble Gentlemen*, we have "Cossar's *two-and-thirty* wounds."—This man, Octavius, has been a standing puzzle and enigma to the historians, from the seeming contradictions of his character. The later writers, however, especially Merivale and Smith, find that the one principle that gave unity to his life and reconciled those contradictions, was a steadfast, inflexible purpose to avenge the murder of his illustrious uncle and adoptive father.

[344] "Till you, traitors as you are, have added the slaughtering of me, another Cæsar, to that of Julius."

[345] *Strain* is *stock*, *lineage*, or *race*; a common use of the word in Shakespeare's time. So in *King Henry V.*, ii. 4: "He is bred out of that bloody *strain* that haunted us in our familiar paths."

CASSIUS. A peevish schoolboy, worthless of such honour,
Join'd with a masker and a reveller![346]
ANTONY. Old Cassius still!
OCTAVIUS. Come, Antony, away!
Defiance, traitors, hurl we in your teeth:
If you dare fight to-day, come to the field;
If not, when you have stomachs.[347]

[*Exeunt* OCTAVIUS, ANTONY, *and their* ARMY.]

CASSIUS. Why, now, blow wind, swell billow and swim bark!
The storm is up, and all is on the hazard.
BRUTUS. Ho, Lucillius! hark, a word with you.
LUCILLIUS. My lord? [BRUTUS *and* LUCILLIUS *converse apart.*]
CASSIUS. Messala,—
MESSALA. What says my general?
CASSIUS. Messala,
This is my birth-day; as this very day
Was Cassius born. Give me thy hand, Messala:
Be thou my witness that against my will,
As Pompey was,[348] am I compell'd to set
Upon one battle all our liberties.
You know that I held Epicurus strong
And his opinion:[349] now I change my mind,
And partly credit things that do presage.
Coming from Sardis, on our former ensign
Two mighty eagles fell, and there they perch'd,
Gorging and feeding from our soldiers' hands;
Who to Philippi here consorted us:
This morning are they fled away and gone;[350]

---

[346] A peevish school-boy, joined with a masker and a reveller, and unworthy even of that honour. The more common meaning of *peevish* was *foolish*.

[347] *Stomach* was often used for *appetite*. Here it means an appetite for *fighting*, of course.

[348] Alluding to the battle of Pharsalia, which took place in the year B.C. 48. Pompey was forced into that battle, against his better judgment, by the inexperienced and impatient men about him, who, inasmuch as they had more than twice Cæsar's number of troops, fancied they could easily crunch him up if they could but meet him. So they tried it, and he quickly crunched up them.

[349] "I was strongly attached to the doctrines of Epicurus." Plutarch has the following in reference to the ghosting of Brutus: "Cassius being in opinion an Epicurean, and reasoning thereon with Brutus, spake to him touching the vision thus: 'In our sect, Brutus, we have an opinion, that we do not always feel or see that which we suppose we do both see and feel, but that our senses, being credulous and therefore easily abused, imagine they see and conjecture that which in truth they do not.'"

[350] When they raised their camp, there came two eagles that, flying with a marvellous force, lighted upon two of the foremost ensigns, and always followed the

And in their steads do ravens, crows and kites,
Fly o'er our heads and downward look on us,
As we were sickly prey: their shadows seem
A canopy most fatal, under which
Our army lies, ready to give up the ghost.
MESSALA. Believe not so.
CASSIUS. I but believe it partly;
For I am fresh of spirit and resolved
To meet all perils very constantly.
BRUTUS. Even so, Lucillius.
CASSIUS. Now, most noble Brutus,
The gods to-day stand friendly, that we may,
Lovers in peace, lead on our days to age!
But since the affairs of men rest still incertain,
Let's reason with[351] the worst that may befall.
If we do lose this battle, then is this
The very last time we shall speak together:
What are you then determined to do?
BRUTUS. Even by the rule of that philosophy
By which I did blame Cato for the death
Which he did give himself;—I know not how,
But I do find it cowardly and vile,
For fear of what might fall, so to prevent
The time of life;[352]—arming myself with patience
To stay the providence of some high powers
That govern us below.
CASSIUS. Then, if we lose this battle,
You are contented to be led in triumph
Thorough the streets of Rome?
BRUTUS. No, Cassius, no: think not, thou noble Roman,
That ever Brutus will go bound to Rome;
He bears too great a mind.[353] But this same day

---

soldiers, which gave them meat and fed them, until they came near to the city of
Philippes; and there, one day only before the battle, they both flew away.—PLUTARCH.

[351] To *reason with* here means to *talk* or *discourse about.* The use of to *reason* for to
converse or *discourse* occurs repeatedly.

[352] *Prevent* is here used in its literal sense of *anticipate.*—By *time* is meant the full
time, the natural period.—To the understanding of this speech, it must be observed, that
the *sense* of the words, "arming myself," &c, follows next after the words, "which he did
give himself."—In this passage, Shakespeare was misled by an error in North's version
of Plutarch, where we have *trust* instead of *trusted.* "Brutus answered him, 'Being yet but
a young man, and not over greatly experienced in the world, I *trust* (I know not how) a
certain rule of philosophy, by the which I did greatly blame Cato for killing himself, as
being no lawful act, touching the gods; nor, concerning men, valiant: but, being now in
the midst of the danger, I am of a contrary mind.'"

[353] The philosopher indeed renounced all confidence in his own principles. He had
adopted them from reading or imitation; they were not the natural growth of instinct or

Must end that work the Ides of March begun;
And whether we shall meet again I know not.
Therefore our everlasting farewell take:
For ever, and for ever, farewell, Cassius!
If we do meet again, why, we shall smile;
If not, why then, this parting was well made.
CASSIUS. For ever, and for ever, farewell, Brutus!
If we do meet again, we'll smile indeed;
If not, 'tis true this parting was well made.
BRUTUS. Why, then, lead on. O, that a man might know
The end of this day's business ere it come!
But it sufficeth that the day will end,
And then the end is known.—Come, ho! away! [*Exeunt.*]

SCENE II.

The Same. The Field of Battle.

[*Alarums. Enter* BRUTUS *and* MESSALA.]

BRUTUS. Ride, ride, Messala, ride, and give these bills
Unto the legions on the other side:[354]
Let them set on at once; for I perceive
But cold demeanor in Octavius' wing,
And sudden push gives them the overthrow.
Ride, ride, Messala: let them all come down. [*Exeunt.*]

SCENE III.

Another part of the field.

[*Alarums. Enter* CASSIUS *and* TITINIUS.]

CASSIUS. O, look, Titinius, look, the villains fly!
Myself have to mine own turn'd enemy:

---

genuine reflection; and, as may easily happen in such a case, his faith in them failed when they were tested by adversity. As long as there seemed a chance that the *godlike stroke* would be justified by success, Brutus claimed the glory of maintaining a righteous cause; but, when all hope fled, he could take leave of philosophy and life together, and exclaim, *I once dreamed that virtue was a thing; I find her only a name, and the mere slave of fortune.* He had blamed Cato for flying from misery by self-murder; but he learnt to justify the same desperate act when he contemplated committing it himself.—MERIVALE.

[354] "The legions on the other side" are those commanded by Cassius; the left wing of the joint army of Brutus and Cassius. Brutus wants Cassius to attack the enemy at the same time that he himself does. In the next scene, Messala and his escort are met by Titinius coming from Cassius.

This ensign here of mine was turning back;
I slew the coward, and did take it[355] from him.
TITINIUS. O Cassius, Brutus gave the word too early;
    Who, having some advantage on Octavius,
    Took it too eagerly: his soldiers fell to spoil,
    Whilst we by Antony are all enclosed.

[*Enter* PINDARUS.]

PINDARUS. Fly further off, my lord, fly further off;
    Mark Antony is in your tents, my lord
    Fly, therefore, noble Cassius, fly far off.
CASSIUS. This hill is far enough.—Look, look, Titinius;
    Are those my tents where I perceive the fire?
TITINIUS. They are, my lord.
CASSIUS. Titinius, if thou lovest me,
    Mount thou my horse, and hide thy spurs in him,
    Till he have brought thee up to yonder troops,[356]
    And here again; that I may rest assured
    Whether yond troops are friend or enemy.
TITINIUS. I will be here again, even with a thought. [*Exit.*]
CASSIUS. Go, Pindarus, get higher on that hill:[357]
    My sight was ever thick; regard Titinius,
    And tell me what thou notest about the field.—

[PINDARUS *goes up.*]

This day I breathed first: time is come round,
And where I did begin, there shall I end;
My life is run his compass.—Sirrah, what news?
PINDARUS. [*Above.*] O my lord!
CASSIUS. What news?
PINDARUS. [*Above.*] Titinius is enclosed round about
    With horsemen, that make to him on the spur;
    Yet he spurs on. Now they are almost on him.—
    Now, Titinius!—Now some 'light.[358] O, he 'lights too.
    He's ta'en. [*Shout.*] and, hark! they shout for joy.
CASSIUS. Come down; behold no more.—

[355] *Ensign* was used, as it is still, either for the flag or for the bearer of it: here it is used for both at once. It was in killing the cowardly ensign that Cassius "to his own turn'd enemy."

[356] "Yonder troops" are Messala and his escort coming from Brutus.

[357] Cassius is now on a hill: he therefore means a hill somewhat *higher* than that he is on.—Cassius was, *in fact*, what we now call *near-sighted.*

[358] Some *alight*, or *dismount.*

O, coward that I am, to live so long,
To see my best friend ta'en before my face!—

[PINDARUS *descends.*]

Come hither, sirrah:
In Parthia did I take thee prisoner;
And then I swore thee, saving of thy life,
That whatsoever I did bid thee do,
Thou shouldst attempt it. Come now, keep thine oath;
Now be a freeman: and with this good sword,
That ran through Cæsar's bowels, search this bosom.
Stand not to answer: here, take thou the hilts;[359]
And, when my face is cover'd, as 'tis now,
Guide thou the sword.—Cæsar, thou art revenged,
Even with the sword that kill'd thee.[360] [*Dies.*]
PINDARUS. So, I am free; yet would not so have been,
  Durst I have done my will. O Cassius,
  Far from this country Pindarus shall run,
  Where never Roman shall take note of him. [*Exit.*]

[*Re-enter* TITINIUS *with* MESSALA.]

MESSALA. It is but change,[361] Titinius; for Octavius
  Is overthrown by noble Brutus' power,
  As Cassius' legions are by Antony.
TITINIUS. These tidings will well comfort Cassius.
MESSALA. Where did you leave him?
TITINIUS. All disconsolate,
  With Pindarus his bondman, on this hill.
MESSALA. Is not that he t hat lies upon the ground?
TITINIUS. He lies not like the living. O my heart!
MESSALA. Is not that he?
TITINIUS. No, this was he, Messala,
  But Cassius is no more.—O setting Sun,
  As in thy red rays thou dost sink to-night,
  So in his red blood Cassius' day is set;
  The sun of Rome is set! Our day is gone;
  Clouds, dews, and dangers come; our deeds are done!
  Mistrust of my success hath done this deed.

---

[359] *Hilts*, plural, for *hilt* was the common usage in the Poet's time. So too with *funerals*, later in this play.

[360] It was a *dagger*, not a sword, that Cassius stabbed Cæsar with. But the same *weapon* is put for the same *owner*; a common figure of speech.

[361] That is, *interchange* of victory and defeat.

MESSALA. Mistrust of good success hath done this deed.
O hateful error, melancholy's child,
Why dost thou show to the apt thoughts of men
The things that are not?[362] O error, soon conceived,
Thou never comest unto a happy birth,
But kill'st the mother that engender'd thee!
TITINIUS. What, Pindarus! where art thou, Pindarus?
MESSALA. Seek him, Titinius, whilst I go to meet
The noble Brutus, thrusting this report
Into his ears; I may say, thrusting it;
For piercing steel and darts envenomed
Shall be as welcome to the ears of Brutus
As tidings of this sight.
TITINIUS. Hie you, Messala,
And I will seek for Pindarus the while.—[*Exit* MESSALA.]
Why didst thou send me forth, brave Cassius?
Did I not meet thy friends? and did not they
Put on my brows this wreath of victory,
And bid me give it thee? Didst thou not hear their shouts?
Alas, thou hast misconstrued every thing!
But, hold thee, take this garland on thy brow;
Thy Brutus bid me give it thee, and I
Will do his bidding.—Brutus, come apace,
And see how I regarded Caius Cassius.—
By your leave, gods:—this is a Roman's part
Come, Cassius' sword, and find Titinius' heart. [*Dies.*]

[*Alarums. Re-enter* MESSALA, *with* BRUTUS, *young* CATO,
STRATO, VOLUMNIUS, *and* LUCILLIUS.]

BRUTUS. Where, where, Messala, doth his body lie?
MESSALA. Lo, yonder, and Titinius mourning it.
BRUTUS. Titinius' face is upward.
CATO. He is slain.
BRUTUS. O Julius Cæsar, thou art mighty yet!
Thy spirit walks abroad and turns our swords
In our own proper entrails.[363] [*Low alarums.*]

---

[362] Cassius is said to have been of a highly choleric or bilious temperament; as such, predisposed to melancholy, and hence apt to be taken with imaginary evils, or to construe things to the worst.

[363] Brutus here strikes the proper key-note of the play. The matter is well stated by Mr. Froude: "The murderers of Cæsar, and those who had either instigated them secretly or applauded them afterwards, were included in a proscription list, drawn by retributive justice on the model of Sulla's. Such of them as were in Italy were immediately killed. Those in the provinces, as if with the curse of Cain upon their heads, came one by one to miserable ends. In three years the tyrannicides of the Ides of March, with their aiders and

CATO. Brave Titinius!
    Look, whether he have not crown'd dead Cassius!
BRUTUS. Are yet two Romans living such as these?—
    The last of all the Romans, fare thee well!
    It is impossible that ever Rome
    Should breed thy fellow.—Friends, I owe more tears
    To this dead man than you shall see me pay.—
    I shall find time, Cassius, I shall find time.—
    Come, therefore, and to Thasos send his body:
    His funerals shall not be in our camp,
    Lest it discomfort us.[364] Lucillius, come;—
    And come, young Cato;—let us to the field.—
    Labeo and Flavius,[365] set our battles on:—
    'Tis three o'clock; and, Romans, yet ere night
    We shall try fortune in a second fight.[366] [*Exeunt.*]

SCENE IV.

Another Part of the Field.

[*Alarums. Enter, fighting,* SOLDIERS *of both* ARMIES; *then*
BRUTUS, *young* CATO, LUCILLIUS, *and others.*]

BRUTUS. Yet, countrymen, O, yet hold up your heads!
CATO. What bastard doth not?[367] Who will go with me?
    I will proclaim my name about the field.—
    I am the son of Marcus Cato, ho!
    A foe to tyrants, and my country's friend;
    I am the son of Marcus Cato, ho! [*Charges the enemy.*]
BRUTUS. And I am Brutus, Marcus Brutus, I;
    Brutus, my country's friend; know me for Brutus!

[*Exit, charging the enemy. Young* CATO *is overpowered, and*

---

abettors, were all dead; some killed in battle, some in prison, some dying by their own hand."

[364] So when he was come thither, after he had lamented the death of Cassius, calling him the last of all the Romans, being impossible that Rome should ever breed again so noble and valiant a man as he, he caused his body to be buried, and sent it to the city of Thassos, fearing lest his funerals within his camp should cause great disorder.— PLUTARCH.

[365] These two men are not named among the persons of the drama, because they speak nothing. Labeo was one of the stabbers of Cæsar; and it is related that when he saw that all was lost, having dug his own grave, he enfranchised a slave, and then thrust a weapon in his hand to kill him.

[366] The Poet very judiciously represents both battles as occurring the same day. They were *in fact* separated by an interval of twenty days.

[367] Meaning, of course, "Who is such a bastard as not to do so?"

falls.]

LUCILLIUS. O young and noble Cato, art thou down?
    Why, now thou diest as bravely as Titinius;
    And mayst be honour'd, being Cato's son.[368]
FIRST SOLDIER. Yield, or thou diest.
LUCILLIUS. Only I yield to die:
    There is so much that thou wilt kill me straight;

    [*Offering money.*]

    Kill Brutus, and be honour'd in his death.
FIRST SOLDIER. We must not. A noble prisoner!
SECOND SOLDIER. Room, ho! Tell Antony, Brutus is ta'en.
FIRST SOLDIER. I'll tell the news. Here comes the general.—

    [*Enter* ANTONY.]

    Brutus is ta'en, Brutus is ta'en, my lord.
ANTONY. Where is he?
LUCILLIUS. Safe, Antony; Brutus is safe enough:
    I dare assure thee that no enemy
    Shall ever take alive the noble Brutus:
    The gods defend him from so great a shame!
    When you do find him, or alive or dead,
    He will be found like Brutus, like himself.
ANTONY. [*to First Soldier.*] This is not Brutus, friend; but, I assure
    you,
    A prize no less in worth: keep this man safe;
    Give him all kindness: I had rather have
    Such men my friends than enemies. Go on,
    And see whether Brutus be alive or dead;
    And bring us word unto Octavius' tent
    How every thing is chanced. [*Exeunt.*]

---

[368] There was the son of Marcus Cato slain, valiantly fighting among the lusty youth. For notwithstanding that he was very weary and over-harried, yet would he not therefore fly, but manfully fighting and laying about him, telling aloud his name, and also his father's name, at length he was beaten down amongst many other dead bodies of his enemies which he had slain round about him.—PLUTARCH.

SCENE V.

Another Part of the Field.

[*Enter* BRUTUS, DARDANIUS, CLITUS, STRATO, *and* VOLUMNIUS.]

BRUTUS. Come, poor remains of friends, rest on this rock.

[BRUTUS *sits.* STRATO *falls asleep.*]

CLITUS. Statillius show'd the torch-light, but, my lord,
  He came not back: he is or ta'en or slain.[369]
BRUTUS. Sit thee down, Clitus: slaying is the word;
  It is a deed in fashion. Hark thee, Clitus. [*Whispers him.*]
CLITUS. What, I, my lord? No, not for all the world.
BRUTUS. Peace then! no words.
CLITUS. I'll rather kill myself.
BRUTUS. Hark thee, Dardanius. [*Whispers him.*]
DARDANIUS. Shall I do such a deed?
CLITUS. O Dardanius!
DARDANIUS. O Clitus!
CLITUS. What ill request did Brutus make to thee?
DARDANIUS. To kill him, Clitus. Look, he meditates.
CLITUS. Now is that noble vessel full of grief,
  That it runs over even at his eyes.
BRUTUS. Come hither, good Volumnius; list a word.
VOLUMNIUS. What says my lord?
BRUTUS. Why, this, Volumnius:
  The ghost of Cæsar hath appear'd to me
  Two several times by night; at Sardis once,
  And, this last night, here in Philippi fields:
  I know my hour is come.[370]

---

[369] Brutus thought that there was no great number of men slain in battle; and, to know the truth of it, there was one called Statilius that promised to go through his enemies, for otherwise it was impossible to go see their camp; and from thence, if all were well, that he would lift up a torch-light in the air, and then return with speed to him. The torch-light was lift up as he had promised, for Statilius went thither. Now Brutus, seeing Statilius tarry long after that, said, "If Statilius be alive, he will come again." But his evil fortune was such that, as he came back, he lighted in his enemies' hands and was slain.—PLUTARCH.

[370] So the Poet read in Plutarch: "The second battle being at hand, this spirit appeared again unto him, but spake never a word. Thereupon Brutus, knowing that he should die, did put himself to all hazard in battle, but yet fighting could not be slain."— Merivale has a strong sentence on this point: "The legend that when preparing for the

VOLUMNIUS. Not so, my lord.
BRUTUS. Nay, I am sure it is, Volumnius.
Thou seest the world, Volumnius, how it goes;
Our enemies have beat us to the pit: [*Low alarums.*]
It is more worthy to leap in ourselves,
Than tarry till they push us. Good Volumnius,
Thou know'st that we two went to school together:
Even for that our love of old, I prithee,
Hold thou my sword-hilts, whilst I run on it.
VOLUMNIUS. That's not an office for a friend, my lord.

[*Alarum still.*]

CLITUS. Fly, fly, my lord; there is no tarrying here.
BRUTUS. Farewell to you;—and you;—and you, Volumnius.—
Strato, thou hast been all this while asleep;

[STRATO *awakes.*]

Farewell to thee too, Strato.—Countrymen,
My heart doth joy that yet in all my life
I found no man but he was true to me.
I shall have glory by this losing day
More than Octavius and Mark Antony
By this vile conquest shall attain unto.
So fare you well at once; for Brutus' tongue
Hath almost ended his life's history:
Night hangs upon mine eyes; my bones would rest,
That have but labour'd to attain this hour.

[*Alarum. Cry within,* Fly, fly, fly!]

CLITUS. Fly, my lord, fly.
BRUTUS. Hence! I will follow.[371]—

---

encounter with the triumvirs he was visited by the ghost of Cæsar, which summoned him
to meet again at Philippi, marks the conviction of the ancients that in the crisis of his fate
he was stung by guilty remorse, and haunted by the presentiment of final retribution."
    [371] Volumnius denied his request, and so did many others; and, amongst the rest,
one of them said, there was no tarrying for them there, but that they must needs fly. Then
Brutus, rising up, "We must fly indeed," said he, "but it must be with our hands, not with
our feet." Then, taking every man by the hand, he said these words unto them with a
cheerful countenance: "It rejoiceth my heart, that not one of my friends hath failed me at
my need, and I do not complain of my fortune, but only for my country's sake: for, as for
me, I think myself happier than they that have overcome, considering that I leave a
perpetual fame of virtue and honesty, the which our enemies the conquerors shall never
attain unto by force or money." Having so said, he prayed every man to shift for himself,

[*Exeunt* CLITUS, DARDANIUS, *and* VOLUMNIUS.]

I prithee, Strato, stay thou by thy lord:
Thou art a fellow of a good respect;[372]
Thy life hath had some smatch of honour in it:
Hold then my sword, and turn away thy face,
While I do run upon it. Wilt thou, Strato?
STRATO. Give me your hand first. Fare you well, my lord.
BRUTUS. Farewell, good Strato.—Cæsar, now be still:
I kill'd not thee with half so good a will.

[*He runs on his sword, and dies.*]

[*Alarums. Retreat. Enter* OCTAVIUS, ANTONY, MESSALA,
LUCILLIUS, *and the* ARMY.]

OCTAVIUS. What man is that?
MESSALA. My master's man.—Strato, where is thy master?
STRATO. Free from the bondage you are in, Messala:
The conquerors can but make a fire of him;
For Brutus only overcame himself,
And no man else hath honour by his death.
LUCILLIUS. So Brutus should be found.—I thank thee, Brutus,
That thou hast proved Lucillius' saying true.
OCTAVIUS. All that served Brutus, I will entertain them.[373]—
[*to* STRATO.] Fellow, wilt thou bestow thy time with me?
STRATO. Ay, if Messala will prefer[374] me to you.
OCTAVIUS. Do so, good Messala.
MESSALA. How died my master, Strato?
STRATO. I held the sword, and he did run on it.
MESSALA. Octavius, then take him to follow thee,
That did the latest service to my master.
ANTONY. This was the noblest Roman of them all:
All the conspirators save only he
Did that they did in envy of great Cæsar;
He only, in a general honest thought

---

and then he went a little aside with two or three only, among the which Strato was one,
with whom he came first acquainted by the study of rhetoric. Strato, at his request, held
the sword in his hand, and turned his head aside, and Brutus fell down upon it, and so ran
himself through, and died presently.—PLUTARCH.

[372] A fellow *well esteemed*, or of good *reputation.* See page 23, note 41.

[373] "I will take them into my service." So in *The Two Gentlemen*, ii. 4 . "Sweet lady,
entertain him for your servant."

[374] *Prefer* was a common term for *recommending* a servant.

And common good[375] to all, made one of them.
His life was gentle, and the elements
So mix'd in him,[376] that Nature might stand up
And say to all the world *This was a man!*
OCTAVIUS. According to his virtue let us use him,
With all respect and rites of burial.
Within my tent his bones to-night shall lie,
Most like a soldier, order'd honourably.
So call the field to rest; and let's away,
To part the glories of this happy day. [*Exeunt.*]

THE END

---

[375] The force of *in* is, properly, continued over *common good.*

[376] Referring to the old doctrine of the four elements, as they were called, earth, water, air, and fire, the right mixing and tempering of which was supposed to be the principle of all excellence in Nature. The Poet has a number of allusions to the doctrine, which was a commonplace of the time. The sense of the word *elements* has so changed as to make the passage just as true to the ideas of our time, as it was to those of three hundred years ago. A rather curious fact.

63539467R00068

Made in the USA
San Bernardino, CA
19 December 2017